MAKING ¢ENT$ OF RETIREMENT PLANS

AN EMPLOYER'S GUIDE

Also by James McSweeney

I $ee The Benefit
An HR Treasure Chest

Making Ȼent$ of Investing
A Guide To Investments and Retirement

Making Cent$ of Retirement Plans

AN EMPLOYER'S GUIDE

By

James J. McSweeney

&

Robert F. McGowan

Comprehensive Benefit Services, Inc.

USA

Making Cent$ of Retirement Plans

Copyright © 2016

By

James J. McSweeney

&

Robert F. McGowan

This book may be ordered through booksellers everywhere, or by contacting:

Comprehensive Benefit Services, Inc.

http://www.askcip.com   admin@askcip.com

ISBN – 13: 978-0-9848683-2-2 (pbk)

ISBN – 13: 978-0-9848683-3-9 (ebk)

Printed in the United States of America

Authors' Note:

The CIP companies service the benefits for thousands of clients across the country.

While helping employers and fiduciaries choose, design and manage retirement plans we realized that our clients needed a good, easy-to-use retirement guide that simplified the process. *Making Cent$ of Retirement Plans* is that book.

Successful 401(k)s are part science and part art. This book is part of the solution. A companion book, entitled *Making Cent$ of Investing* finishes the job.

When used together, employers will have all they need to create dramatic improvements to any retirement plan.

Note: A portion of this book draws upon on of the author's prior work, *I $ee The Benefit: An HR Treasure Chest*.

Dedication

This book is dedicated to all of the people behind the scenes that make the CIP companies run smoothly.

First, we would like to thank our families. Without support from home, we could never succeed as we do.

Second, we would like to thank our employees. Few individuals understand the complexity of today's regulations. For every objective, there are obstacles in the way. Clients don't see the dedication it takes to perform your jobs to near-perfection every day. We do.

Finally, we would like to thank all the vendors, record keepers, plan administrators, actuaries, tech specialists, fiduciaries, financial regulators and service people that help us serve clients to the best of our ability.

CONTENTS

PART ONE:

THE RETIREMENT PLAN LANDSCAPE

PART TWO:

HUMAN NATURE

PART THREE:
BUILDING THE OPTIMAL 401(K)

FOREWORD

It is no secret that everyone needs to save for retirement. Without adequate savings, retirees must rely upon the government, their families and charities for support.

Americans are not saving enough. They invest poorly.

Most retirees depend on Social Security for over half of their retirement income. Over one third of "retirement" income comes from *working* wages.

The government is deeply in debt. Social Security is highly flawed. The traditional nuclear family is history. Supportive charities are struggling for donations.

The retirees of tomorrow must be able to support themselves. Everyone knows this. Wealth accumulation is high on everybody's "to do" list. So, why can't people save and invest effectively? There are many reasons. Most of them can be fixed — especially by employers.

Perhaps you are an employer who continually struggles to convince employees to participate in your 401(k)... Perhaps you are an executive who can't save enough, despite your best intentions... Maybe you are a business owner looking to save more in a tax-favored manner...

Whatever your goals, there are proven methods that companies can use to dramatically increase retirement saving and wealth accumulation.

This book explains each retirement planning strategy that employers can implement — for themselves and for their employees. Whichever plan, or combination of plans, you choose will depend upon your personal and corporate goals.

DEDUCTIBILITY STRINGS

Most retirement plans allow employers to deduct contributions made for employees. This deductibility comes with strings that are imposed by Congress.

Retirement plans must be "fair," and provide practically equal benefits for all employees. Congress sets the limits. Smart employers (especially private companies) learn how to manage deductibility limits for their benefit. Company contributions can often be skewed toward the ownership and executive groups, while still maintaining legal fairness and deductibility.

It is not unusual for private companies to direct 80-90% of company contributions to the executive group, and still be fair under the law.

Some retirement plan strategies, such as deferred compensation, may not be fully tax-deductible to employers. These plans can still be attractive, especially if a company wants to create benefits for specific individuals, such as key employees.

Certain retirement plans, such as 401(k), allow individuals to save for themselves. These plans may or may not involve a matching contribution. They often do, since appropriate matching allows for lower administration expenses.

A PLANNING PARTNERSHIP

Successful retirement planning is a partnership between employers and their employees.

Employees must take independent steps to save and invest for their futures. Employers can provide extraordinary help. This can often be done in a way that benefits employees, without creating a negative impact to the bottom line. In fact, retirement plans can increase employee productivity and corporate profits.

This book demonstrates how employers can choose, design and manage more effective retirement plans.

NOT A BUDGET PROBLEM

In a Utopian world, employers would have sufficient revenues to provide full retirement savings for their employees. We don't live in Utopia. Every profit dollar is a struggle to earn.

Employers must optimize their resources to build the most effective retirement plans. Most don't. This isn't because employers don't want to. They do. *They just don't know how to get the most from their money and their time.*

LIFE IS COMPLICATED

People are complicated. We are ruled by habits and emotions we don't understand and can't control.

Retirement law is convoluted. The government creates restrictions and regulations that make it challenging for all employers.

Studies have shown that effective education and a proper plan structure can affect human behavior in a positive way — especially when it comes to saving for retirement. When a retirement plan is designed to mesh with human nature, rather than clash against it, dramatic change results.

YOUR HIGHLY TRAINED CONSULTANT

Most small and medium-sized companies don't employ behavioral psychologists to help employees take the steps need-ed to achieve an optimal retirement. Employers can't afford to hire executives with Ph.D.s in human resources. They rely on what their broker or financial advisor says is the best way to go. Some employers simply contact a company that "sells" or "offers" retirement plans and chooses from their menu.

Employers *can* optimize employee saving and cost effective-ness. But they rarely do.

401(k)

401(K) is the most popular type of retirement plan. 401(k)s are cost effective. They give employees an easy forum to plan for retirement on their own.

Unfortunately, most 401(k) plans are not designed to adapt to how employees naturally behave. This book incorporates in-formation learned through controlled human behavioral stud-ies, and ones tested in the field. Then it shows you how to build a better plan.

THE RIGHT COMBINATION

A good 401(k) integrates,

- Academic studies of human nature, with,

- Effective employee education,

- To create a blueprint for the,

- Nuts and bolts of retirement plan design.

When a plan's architecture adapts to human nature, radical im-provements are possible. Employees will save more. They be-come more productive workers. They can grow happier with their lives, and also with their employers.

Most 401(k) plans do not utilize the critical tools and methods that can transform a good plan into a great plan—with little or no added expense.

This book will show you how to re-engineer your 401(k) plan to derive maximum benefit for the company and its employees, all within budget.

If you are self-employed, you will have to read this book as both employer and employee. There is much in here for you, too.

PLAN DESIGN & IMPLEMENTATION

Most 401(k) plans force employees to fight their own natural instincts. Effective participation can only be achieved once these emotional and financial hurdles are managed.

This book gives employers a better understanding of what drives saving and investment decisions.

Creative and intelligent plan administrators can then learn how to implement changes that take full advantage of our *natural* behavior.

These changes will help employees accumulate far more than they do today.

OTHER RETIREMENT STRATEGIES

401(k) is not the only attractive retirement planning vehicle available to companies.

This book helps employers explore other methods that may be more favorable, especially for owners and executives. Some types of plans can be implemented *alongside* a 401(k), to better achieve corporate goals.

Since most businesses in this country are privately owned, this book reviews strategies that can be used to divert more profits into deductible plan contributions for the ownership and executive groups. Such designs can also benefit non-executive employees, providing a win-win for all.

TAXES AND REGULATIONS

Because retirement plans receive favorable tax treatment, they come with restrictions. This book helps sponsors understand and manage the government regulations that constrict the use of retirement vehicles.

EDUCATION

This book is designed to partner with the investment education book entitled, *Making Cent$ of Investing*. This unique guide presents critical investment concepts in a way that employees can understand. It can motivate.

Investment education is everywhere. We view it on television. We get it in the mail. We see it on the bookshelves. We get advice from employers, financial advisors, friends and family members. Everybody has an opinion. The problem is: It doesn't work — at least for most of us. You will need to make it work.

Employers must tie relevant information together, and then present the material in a way that can be easily understood.

The majority of individuals:

- Ignore professional advice,

- Invest poorly, and

- Don't save enough.

This sets people up for painful realizations when it is far too late. Financial tragedy can be avoided. Employers can help.

EFFECTIVE EDUCATION

Effective investment education must *motivate*. This is easy to say. It is challenging to implement. Employers must develop ways to penetrate the barriers that nature puts in the way of knowledge and action.

CHANGING BEHAVIOR

Changes in investment behavior must come from changes *within*. Internal change must come from new knowledge, combined with the personal determination to alter investment behavior.

Change can also come from *employers*. Employers must learn how to design, implement and manage retirement plans more effectively.

THE HUMAN CONDITION

Why don't people save enough for retirement? Why does so much investment advice refuse to take root?

When the onion gets peeled, the answer is simple — Human Nature. Our bodies are hard-wired to make decisions emotionally, not logically. We may back up emotional decisions with logic, but the decisions themselves are driven by feelings.

We do things that make us feel good. We avoid things that make us feel uncomfortable. We make emotional, "gut" reactions that run counter to our intellectual logic. Neuroscience now demonstrates how the gut actually *does* influence behavior. So do many other things that we cannot see. You must learn how they sabotage retirement planning.

PHYSIOLOGY

An understanding of human physiology is critical to helping employees achieve their long-term financial goals. Much of our conscious investment behavior is ruled by the unconscious. Employers must understand these motivators, and design retirement plans that allow the "decision makers within" to make better choices.

Once an individual viscerally understands the concepts of inflation and purchasing power...If a person finally understands the power of compound growth and modern portfolio theory... can they feel more comfortable with a little short-term risk? Absolutely.

VISUALIZE THE FUTURE

Could self-visualization convince an employee to forgo a daily latte and extravagant spending for a little more saving? It actually can.

Scientific studies have shown that *personal* visualization of the future can alter current investment behavior. When we think of ourselves in the future, the chemistry in our brains often "see" ourselves as *someone else*. When we see a picture of our own selves, aged into the future, our brains can make the proper neuro connections and react positively.

An aged self-portrait can literally stimulate the *proper* section of the brain, to increase saving motivation, perhaps by as much as 30%.

Traditional methods, like putting a picture of a future vaca-
tion or retirement home on one's desk, can work as motivating
goals. A trip to a subsidized "retirement home" can also open
eyes to the result of today's inaction — projecting a Scrooge-
like ghost of our retirement future.

There are many ways to make retirement real. Every one of
them can enhance results. You must learn how to implement
them all, and properly.

NUMBERS

Employee education must present numbers and facts. Numbers make sense. Numbers matter. Numbers don't lie. They do
shade the truth, however, if presented improperly or incom-
pletely.

Employers must present critical, retirement planning numbers
without bias, in a meaningful way.

A full understanding of numerical facts can alter one's percep-
tion of reality, in a way that will change investment behavior. Understanding facts can reduce fear. Understanding facts
can create new motivations, ones that are focused less on the
wasteful habits of today, and more in favor of financial security for tomorrow.

The investment education companion to this book, *Making
Cent$ of Investing,* educates in a way that employees can un-
derstand. Most plan providers have developed similar information, but it is not the same. It is critical that employers present education that delivers the message and promotes action.

ACTION

Nothing happens without positive action. Saving can't happen without the conscious decision to save. Meaningful accumulation (investing) can't happen without the decision to undertake risk. Once present and future needs have been quantified...Once the planning methodology and the risks are fully understood...employees can develop a saving and investment strategy that meets their individual financial goals, without causing undue stress.

GOALS

Science has shown that humans are more productive when they have specific, tangible goals. When large goals are set, and then broken into achievable, stair-step actions, big goals become manageable. Short-term sacrifice becomes acceptable when it is part of a greater plan.

THE NUMBER

The NUMBER is a long-term, personal financial goal that can be broken down into manageable steps. Every employee should have a number, a specific, tangible retirement target. See if your plan providers can help each employee set a specific, numerical goal for their retirement accumulation, and then set out to achieve it.

The NUMBER represents financial independence, the destination for each person's retirement GPS system. If we deviate off of our initial route — if inflation, income, expenses, or investment returns don't meet our initial calculations, our system must recalibrate. It determines a new route. The new route may represent more or less saving. It might cause a change in investment philosophy. It could mean working another year or two, even getting a second job or working overtime.

But it gets us there.

The steps to achieving one's number can be started today. These steps will change over time, as circumstances change. Achieving one's number should be an ongoing process that requires focused attention. And it all starts with a plan — often a company retirement plan.

401(k) education should help employees set this target, *and* make it easier for them to attain it.

A PLAN FOR THE UNPREDICTABLE

Nobody can predict the stock market, global economic events and tax rates. No one can guarantee the future of Social Security and Medicare. It is impossible to accurately project future income, health, job security, or the amount that might be needed for education or unexpected expenses. But everyone can plan. Planning is critical.

Employers must make planning simple to understand and easy to do.

DIFFERENT LEARNING

People learn differently. Employers must present education and retirement strategies in different ways — with the hope that each employee will have an Ebenezer Scrooge moment — a clear vision of their future, and a plan to get there.

401(K) SUMMARY

Employees are not saving sufficiently for retirement. There are two major reasons:

- Employers implement less-than-optimal retirement plan designs.

- There is a lack of proper, motivating education provided to employees.

401(K) Enhancements

Employers can adjust plan features, investment options and matching schedules to increase participation and investment accumulation.

Plan sponsors can deliver education that makes it physically and emotionally easier for employees to save more for retirement.

When better employee understanding is combined with better plan design, extraordinary changes can, and will occur.

THIS BOOK'S CONSTRUCTION

1. This book begins with a history of retirement planning. It explains how the tax advantages of various plans are used and regulated. Then it describes the types of plans and strategies that can be used by employers.

2. The second part of this book gives a brief overview of human nature — as it relates to saving and investments. By understanding human nature, employers can build better retirement plans.

3. The final section of the book details optimal 401(k) design and implementation. Why?

    a. 401(k) is the prime retirement vehicle used by employers, and by employees to achieve financial independence.

b. 401(k) is where employees have the most control over their financial well-being.

c. 401(k) is the area where employers do the poorest job.

Most 401(k)s are not designed correctly. They aren't built to accommodate the way people *behave*. Most plans are overpriced for what they deliver.

These flaws cause poor employee participation, and sub-par investment performance by most participants.

EMPLOYER WIN

When employers incorporate behavioral improvements to their plans, they see dramatic improvement in employee participation. Plan improvements also generate better investment returns. This can lead to higher productivity and greater employee well-being.

This book will show you how to design a 401(k) to achieve maximum participation. It will also teach you how to improve plan investment performance.

DOUBLE PLAN PARTICIPATION

With proper 401(k) implementation, it is not unusual for employers to *double* plan participation. Doubling plan deferrals has an extraordinary impact on employee financial security and overall happiness. Make it happen.

repetitio est mater studiorum
Repetition is the mother of studies.

Some concepts in this book will be repeated. This is intentional. Repetition enhances learning. The same holds true with retirement plan education. Important concepts must be repeated until they are learned and internalized.

Let's begin.

Chapter One

R
_____

Retirement Plan Overview

Retirement Plan History

Retirement plans have evolved over the years and will continue to do so. This change has been driven by financial and macroeconomic trends. Plan evolution has also been influenced by social trends that have occurred within the job marketplace.

As business and employee needs change, Congress introduces legislation to meet the goals of both.

Years ago, most Americans worked for large companies. Little changed within those companies, and employees often spent a career working for the same organization. A large company would promise each employee a pension and gold watch at retirement, in exchange for that employee's long-term loyalty to the organization.

With such stability, there was little demand for a diverse array of retirement plans. For many years, there were two types of pension plans. Companies would implement a *Defined Benefit Pension Plan,* a *Money Purchase Pension Plan*, or both. Pension plans were loosely regulated until Congress passed the ERISA legislation in 1974. ERISA established concrete guidelines (and penalties) regarding retirement plan management, eligibility, contribution limits, investments, fiduciary responsibility, etc.

In addition to pensions, companies could also implement a *Profit Sharing Plan,* where employers shared a portion of profits with all employees. These became regulated under ERISA as well.

Since ERISA, Congress has made many changes to retirement plan law. Congress has created new regulations, bringing additional features to traditional plans. Congress also made changes that allowed for new types of plans.

The following chapters highlight the features and benefits of the types of retirement plans that can be offered to employees. The goal here is to:

- Help you choose plans that are right for your company.
- Help you manage your plan(s) more efficiently.
- Help you become better informed about your responsibilities.

RETIREMENT PLAN OVERVIEW

Retirement plans come in many forms. Some are funded completely with company monies, while others are funded solely by employees. Some are negotiated and customized with bargaining units, while many are off-the-shelf plans with no customization at all.

Most private companies have similar objectives when implementing retirement plans. Most employers want to:

- Offer plans that are owner/executive friendly.
    - o Most smaller companies are privately held. When the company contributes to a retirement plan, the contribution comes from money that

would otherwise be retained by ownership.

- Offer plans that attract and retain highly skilled employees.
  - o Businesses cannot afford to lose key employees because they don't remain competitive in the retirement plan marketplace.
  - o Plans should be managed well, and they should offer employees the best possible mix of investment options.

- Minimize plan expenses. This is important for several reasons.
  - o Plan sponsors have a fiduciary responsibility to manage plan expenses.
  - o Employers generally seek to minimize their own out of pocket costs.
  - o Excess plan expenses can reduce investment returns for employees.

- Communicate effectively. Companies want their employees to understand how to make the best use of their retirement choices.

- Minimize fiduciary liability.
  - o Since plan trustees/companies can be held personally liable for breaches in fiduciary duty, owners and executives are particularly attentive to fiduciary risk.

- Minimize plan administration requirements.

- Provide accurate and timely information to the plan trustees and beneficiaries.

Qualified Plans

Retirement plans must qualify for favorable income tax treatment. Plan qualification allows contributions made by an employer to be tax deductible. Qualification also allows plan investments to grow on a tax-deferred basis. Qualification rules vary depending upon the type of plan. We will review these in greater detail later.

The IRS Rules

The Internal Revenue Service is responsible for ensuring compliance with the Internal Revenue Code. The Internal Revenue Code establishes specific rules for operating tax-qualified plans, including plan funding and vesting requirements.

ERISA

Qualified retirement plans are governed by the act of Congress that is known as ERISA. Under ERISA, the U.S. Department of Labor's *Employee Benefits Security Administration* is charged with enforcing the rules governing:

- Plan managers,
- Investment of plan assets,
- Reporting and disclosure of plan information,
- Enforcement of the fiduciary provisions of the law, and
- Workers' benefit rights.

If you are going to sponsor a qualified retirement plan you should understand the law. A copy of the Department of Labor's ERISA explanation is included in this book. Many plan sponsors hear about the law from advisors, but never understand the essence of its rules. Because of its importance and complexity, the exact text of what the DOL has to say about

ERISA is as follows:

"What is ERISA?

"The Employee Retirement Income Security Act of 1974, or ERISA, protects the assets of millions of Americans so that funds placed in retirement plans during their working lives will be there when they retire.

"ERISA is a federal law that sets minimum standards for pension plans in private industry. For example, if an employer maintains a pension plan, ERISA specifies when an employee must be allowed to become a participant, how long they have to work before they have a non-forfeitable interest in their pension, how long a participant can be away from their job before it might affect their benefit, and whether their spouse has a right to part of their pension in the event of their death. Most of the provisions of ERISA are effective for plan years beginning on or after January 1, 1975.

"ERISA does not require any employer to establish a pension plan. It only requires that those who establish plans must meet certain minimum standards. The law generally does not specify how much money a participant must be paid as a benefit.

"ERISA does the following:

"Requires plans to provide participants with information about the plan including important information about plan features and funding. The plan must furnish some information regularly and automatically. Some is available free of charge, some is not.

"Sets minimum standards for participation, vesting, benefit accrual and funding. The law defines how long a person may

be required to work before becoming eligible to participate in a plan, to accumulate benefits, and to have a non-forfeitable right to those benefits. The law also establishes detailed funding rules that require plan sponsors to provide adequate funding for your plan.

"Requires accountability of plan fiduciaries. ERISA generally defines a fiduciary as anyone who exercises discretionary authority or control over a plan's management or assets, including anyone who provides investment advice to the plan. Fiduciaries who do not follow the principles of conduct may be held responsible for restoring losses to the plan.

"Gives participants the right to sue for benefits and breaches of fiduciary duty.

"Guarantees payment of certain benefits if a defined plan is terminated, through a federally chartered corporation, known as the Pension Benefit Guaranty Corporation."

You can read the full text of this explanation at the following Internet location:

http://www.dol.gov/ebsa/faqs/faq_compliance_pension.html

When you think about ERISA, you must understand that this law has teeth the size of a bear. Unfortunately, abiding by every ERISA statute requires the wisdom of Solomon and the patience of Job. None of us are perfect, but you must do everything in your power to abide by ERISA's regulations.

FIDUCIARY RULES

If you are a retirement plan trustee, or a business owner, you will (almost always) be considered a plan *fiduciary*. Plan fiduciaries have specific obligations under the law. If you breach these responsibilities, the Department of Labor may hold you *personally liable* for asset losses in your plan, even if the assets are self-directed.

Here is what the Department of Labor has to say about fiduciary responsibility:

"The Employee Retirement Income Security Act (ERISA) protects your plan's assets by requiring that those persons or entities who exercise discretionary control or authority over plan management or plan assets, anyone with discretionary authority or responsibility for the administration of a plan, or anyone who provides investment advice to a plan for compensation or has any authority or responsibility to do so are subject to fiduciary responsibilities. Plan fiduciaries include, for example, plan trustees, plan administrators, and members of a plan's investment committee.

"The primary responsibility of fiduciaries is to run the plan solely in the interest of participants and beneficiaries and for the exclusive purpose of providing benefits and paying plan expenses. Fiduciaries must act prudently and must diversify the plan's investments in order to minimize the risk of large losses. In addition, they must follow the terms of plan documents to the extent that the plan terms are consistent with ERISA. They also must avoid conflicts of interest. In other words, they may not engage in transactions on behalf of the plan that benefit parties related to the plan, such as other fiduciaries, services providers or the plan sponsor.

"Fiduciaries who do not follow these principles of conduct may be personally liable to restore any losses to the plan, or to restore any profits made through improper use of plan assets. Courts may take whatever action is appropriate against fiduciaries who breach their duties under ERISA including their removal."

You can read the full text of this explanation at the following Internet location:

http://www.dol.gov/dol/topic/retirement/fiduciaryresp.htm

Note: Private retirement plans are regulated under Title I of ERISA, which is enforced by the U.S. Department of Labor. Plans run by public entities — such as federal, state and local governments — may not be governed under Title I of the law.

Summary

You've now got a general view of retirement plans and their regulation. It is time to discuss the particulars of plans that you may offer to employees.

As you read about the various plan structures, you will find that certain ones, and their variations, provide significant advantages. Depending upon your objectives, you will choose the one plan, or a combination of plans, that will best satisfy your needs.

As we go along, you should begin to understand your legal responsibilities regarding plan management, as well as the tax implications of any plan you choose.

Chapter Two

R

Defined Benefit Pension Plans

Defined Benefit Pensions

Defined benefit pensions pay employees a benefit that is *defined* at retirement. With this type of plan, an employer tells employees: "If you work for our company for X number of years, and you earn Y, we promise to pay you Z..."

An employee's benefit under any plan is determined by a formula. Formulas are flexible at the creation of a plan. Typically, the employer agrees to pay retirees a certain percentage of their salary (or total compensation), adjusted by the number of years of service with the company. Most employers pay a higher retirement benefit to employees with the longest company tenure. It often takes many years of employment before an employee earns a meaningful pension at retirement.

Once a formula has been chosen, great care must be taken if you decide to change it. Formulas are easy to make and hard to break.

In a typical defined benefit pension plan, an employee with

thirty years of service might expect to retire (at age 65) with 40%-80% of their final salary. This is usually in addition to Social Security and other benefits — provided the company is still in business and the pension has been fully funded.

A typical benefit formula might credit employees 2% of pay for each year worked with the company. Under this formula, an employee who has worked with the company for 35 years would receive 70% of pay at retirement. Pay (in this example) is defined as the *average total income* for the last *three years* of service with the company. If the average income is $100,000, this retiree will receive $70,000 per year in retirement. There may also be a cost of living adjustment included, where benefits increase over time with inflation.

Benefit formulas might pay 1%, 1.5%, or 2.5% per year. They might cap retirement pay at 50% or 60% of compensation. Some might cap benefits at 20 years' of service, 25 years, or 35 years. Final pay formulas can also be customized. The variations are flexible and can be mixed and matched, depending upon the goals of the company.

Payout

Under current law, the most that an employee may receive as a defined benefit retirement income is $210,000 per year.

Payments at retirement are typically made on a monthly basis. Some plans allow for a lump sum payment in lieu of monthly benefits. The lump sum payment would be determined by the plan's actuaries. The amount paid will normally be the *present value* of the *future benefits*. This is the sum of cash that it would take, today, to provide the promised future benefits. This formula is a function of the employee's age, benefit and the prevailing interest rates in the financial marketplace.

If you pay attention to lottery winners, you will notice that some of them choose to receive annual payments. Others choose an "equivalent lump sum" payment. The lump sum payment is significantly lower than the sum of the annual payments. This is because the lump sum can be invested to earn a rate of return, which (in theory) would ultimately equal the sum of the monthly payments.

When an employee leaves a company *before* retirement, they may be entitled to a current lump sum payment from a defined benefit plan. The plan may also keep the money, continue to invest it, and pay the employee in the normal manner at retirement. The amount that an employee is "owed" by the plan will be the present value of the vested benefits. We will review both of these concepts shortly.

Vesting in a Defined Benefit Plan

There are legal regulations that require employees to become "vested" in benefits provided under defined benefit retirement plans. Vested benefits are *owned* by the employee, and *owed* by the plan.

Vesting in defined benefit plans is fairly complicated. Your retirement plan administrator should be able to explain the particulars of any plan. Essentially, employees become vested in their benefits, as earned.

If a plan is terminated, employees will become immediately and fully vested in their benefits.

Present Value

If an employee leaves a company before retirement, the plan owes the employee the *present value* of the vested *future benefit*. This benefit may be less than the money already put into the plan to fund it. This is because a plan funds, today, to pay the full vested benefit, given a rate of return, years in the future.

If an employee leaves a company after a relatively short period of time, much of the money that has been set aside for the retirement benefit may come **back to the plan**.

Here is a simplified example: An employee has worked for a company from age 20 to 25. He is fully vested in his benefit, and has been earning $20,000 per year. The employee has been credited with 2% of pay each year. Therefore, he is vested in 10% (2% for five years) of $20,000. The plan owes this employee $2,000 per year *forty years* from now, for life.

How much does the plan actually owe this employee today? The amount owed today is the present value of the future benefit, which is $2,000 per year in forty years.

How much cash will it take to provide this benefit? ERISA law gives ranges of returns that actuaries are allowed to assume for rate of return calculations. Your actuary will choose a rate from within this range (which is derived from historical interest rates) and use a prevailing life expectancy table to determine the present value of the future benefit. For simplicity, let's assume that your actuary determines that 5% is a reasonable return on investments. $40,000 invested at 5% would yield $2,000 per year today. Your actuary will also calculate for a reduction in principal over the employee's expected lifetime. This may reduce the $40,000 to a lower figure, because the $2,000 benefit would be calculated only for the employee's life expectancy, about 20 years. Let's say that your actuary reduces this future amount to $35,000.

$5,000 invested today, at 5% per year, would grow to $35,200 forty years from now. Therefore, the *present value* of the benefit earned by your 5-year employee is about $5,000. This is what your plan would owe this employee with five years of service.

In order to fund the full retirement benefit of this employee, you may have set aside $2,000 per year. The money may have grown to $12,000. Therefore, you would segregate the **$5,000** that is *vested* by your employee. This may or may not be paid today, depending upon your plan document. The balance of **$7,000** would ***revert*** to your plan.

Defined Benefit in Private Business

Defined benefit plans can be extremely attractive to private businesses, particularly if they have older owners who want to set aside larger sums of money than are allowed by traditional retirement plans. Six-figure plan contributions for key employees and owners are not uncommon.

$&¢

Chapter Three

R

Money Purchase Pension Plans

Money Purchase Pensions

With a money purchase pension, a company guarantees to make pension contributions for all eligible employees, such as 5%, 10%, or 15% of pay each year. These funds are often held in a pooled account which is managed by advisors hired by the company. Independent, third party administration firms are hired to keep track of how much is in the account for each employee.

Some employers allow employees to take control over their own investments, in a manner similar to 401(k) accounts. 401(k)s are explained in a later chapter.

As business has become more competitive and less predictable, large companies have been migrating away from defined benefit and money purchase pension plans. Employers are less able to make long-term commitments to pension accounts.

Many defined benefit pension plans, particularly those for union employees, such as laborers and state workers, are in significant financial trouble. Because of these financial challenges, employees have become less willing to stake their financial futures on a forty-year promise made by a company that might not exist when the time comes to retire.

As the use of traditional pension plans has subsided, the use of other forms of retirement plans has grown substantially. We examine additional plan options in the following chapters.

Chapter Four

_____R_____

Cash Balance Plans

Cash Balance Plans

Many companies have migrated from traditional, defined benefit pension plans toward the use of Cash Balance Pension Plans. These plans use funding formulas similar to defined benefit pension plans. But companies are not obligated to make a thirty or forty year promise. Companies make annual contributions for employees. Contributions are made into employee-controlled accounts, based upon defined-benefit-type formulas. Employees assume the investment risk. They may be subject to vesting in their investment accounts. The company (plan sponsor) is *not* obligated to continue future funding if business conditions change. They can cease funding the plan after sufficient employee notice.

This hybrid pension reduces the liability of long-term funding. It also gives employees tangible assets that can't be forfeited, provided they hold up their end of the loyalty bargain by remaining with the company.

$&¢

Chapter Five

R

Profit Sharing Plans

Profit Sharing Plans

Profit Sharing Plans are the retirement plan cornerstone for most American companies. Profit sharing plans do not create the same long-term liabilities for employers as pension plans. Contributions do not have to be made after every year. They are made at the employer's discretion. In addition, employees do not accrue future benefits, simply by working another year for the company. In a competitive and uncertain business climate, this is a more attractive option for most employers.

Employers establish profit sharing plans as an incentive to attract and retain productive employees. Contributions are made from company profits, although contributions can still be made in a money-losing year.

A ten or fifteen percent (of salary) annual profit sharing contribution can be a powerful incentive for employees to see that a company remains profitable.

Deductible contributions to profit sharing plans are limited by tax laws. The maximum annual company contribution to a plan is twenty-five percent of payroll. The individual limitations are detailed in a later chapter.

Note: There are variations to profit sharing formulas that can be advantageous to the owners and executives of smaller businesses. This book will review these as well.

Chapter Six

_____R_____

401(K)

401(k)

In the late 1970s, Congress reacted to the changing business marketplace by adding an *employee-deferral feature* to the traditional profit sharing plan. Deferral profit sharing plans became known as 401(k) plans, because they utilize sub-section (k) of Section 401 of the Internal Revenue Code. The first plan using the employee-deferral concept was created in 1981.

Insurance companies dominated the early 401(k) marketplace, particularly for private businesses. An insurance company would choose a set of mutual funds from several fund families (typically ten to forty funds) and place them inside a *group annuity* contract. They would then add an asset charge on top of the normal mutual fund fees (typically 1% - 2%) to cover their expenses. Asset charges have grown smaller over time.

Insurance companies still offer some of the most competitive 401(k) plans.

The earliest *mutual fund* 401(k) programs consisted of funds offered solely by the sponsoring mutual fund company. For example, if an employer put their 401(k) plan with Company Z, the employer could choose from Company Z funds only for their plan.

In the 1990s, the nation's first *Open Architecture* 401(k) was created. Open architecture allowed employers to choose from thousands of investment options for their plan. This let employers offer the best mix of investment choices, while dramatically reducing plan administration expenses.

Open architecture also allowed for the use of individual brokerage accounts by plan participants.

The earliest open architecture 401(k)s were built by independent third party administrators (TPAs). A company (plan sponsor) would hire a TPA who would work with an independent investment specialist to create a completely customized plan.

Mutual fund and insurance companies were quick to embrace open architecture. It allowed these providers to expand investment offerings, and reduce overall expenses.

Today, virtually all plans offered by TPAs, mutual fund companies and insurance companies utilize some variation of the open architecture concept.

How a 401(k) Works

A 401(k) is a "qualified" plan that receives favorable tax treatment under the law. In order to remain qualified, the plan must follow a complex set of regulations. The focus of these laws is to ensure that the plan does not discriminate against any group of employees.

The Essence of 401(k)

If you work in company management, you already know that a 401(k) is one of the most popular benefits that can be offered to employees.

MISPERCEPTION

There is a common misperception that 401(k)s are expensive, particularly for small employers. This is not the case. A 401(k) can be offered at little or no direct cost to any company.

Another misconception is that employees won't participate. They will, particularly if employees are educated properly.

Don't avoid implementing a 401(k) because you think you can't afford it, or that your employees won't use it, even if they tell you they won't. Affordable plans are available to any company. Nearly all employees participate, once they are properly educated.

As a retirement plan executive, you should know how a 401(k) works. You should understand your responsibilities, and what you must do to fulfill your duties in managing the plan. Here is a list of the key features of any 401(k).

- A 401(k) is a profit sharing plan with an employee salary-deferral feature.
- The plan sponsor (company) nominates trustees, usually the business owner & company executives, to establish the plan for employees.
- The plan trustees become Fiduciaries — with specific requirements and liabilities for breach of duty.
  - o Fiduciaries are entrusted with seeing that the plan does not discriminate in favor of certain

employees, and that the management of the plan is made for the welfare of its participants.

- o Fiduciary obligations involve aspects of employee education, plan administration, cost control and disclosure.

- o Most plan providers can help execute fiduciary obligations in a low-stress manner.

- An *Investment Policy Statement* must be prepared by the plan trustees. Think of this as a business plan for your 401(k).

- *Individual accounts* are established for all participating employees.

  - o The company withholds a percentage of employee income (as determined by each employee) and contributes it to the plan.

- A third party administrator (TPA) is hired to manage the *accounting* and *recordkeeping* for the plan. The plan TPA may be completely independent. A TPA may be owned by the 401(k) provider. Or, the TPA may be specifically contracted by a 401(k) provider to do the work.

- A company is hired to *manage* the investments (usually mutual funds).

  - o An advisor is engaged by the plan trustees to help manage Fiduciary obligations.

  - o The advisor helps the trustees choose investments for the plan.

  - o The advisor usually helps with the Investment Policy Statement.

  - o The adviser usually educates employees regarding the plan and its investments.

- Employees typically determine where their individual funds will be invested.

- The investment company and the TPA provide accurate *information* regarding plan investments.

- Employees are allowed to *change* their allocations regularly (daily in some plans).

- *Eligibility* is determined by the plan.
  - o Under most circumstances, employees that are over the age of 21, with a full year of service (1,000 hours), must be included in the plan.

- The *average* deferral percentage of highly compensated employees (HCEs) may not exceed 2% more than the average deferral percentage of non-highly compensated employees.

- The plan sponsor (your company) can *match* employee contributions.
  - o Matching contributions will be determined by a customized formula.
  - o Company matches can have a *vesting* schedule.

- Specific rules *regulate* how much of the company *contributions* can be allocated toward the ownership/executive group.
  - o Limits to highly compensated employees (HCEs) are based upon company ownership and income levels.

- Additional *profit sharing* contributions can be made to the plan.

- *Loans* can be made available to plan participants.

Loans are secured by employee funds only. These will be subject to certain limitations.

- *Hardship withdrawals* can be allowed from employee accounts in the plan. These will be subject to limitations.

- Employee contributions into a 401(k) are typically *tax deductible* when going in. Please note that certain states may still tax employee deferrals.

- Investments grow on a *tax deferred* basis.

- Employee deferrals are still subject to *Medicare and Social Security taxes.*

- When distributions are made from the plan (or any subsequent IRA), all proceeds (from most plans) will be subject to *income taxation.*

- Sometimes, company stock can be distributed on a more tax-favorable basis.

In a ***Roth 401(k),*** contributions are made on an *after tax basis.* The investments grow on a *tax-free* basis and come out *tax free*. We will discuss the details of a Roth 401(k) soon.

Chapter Seven

R

401(K) Rules

401(k) RULES:

Contribution Limits:

The government sets limits on how much can be contributed annually to any retirement plan, including a 401(k).

With a 401(k), these limits consist of maximum annual contributions by employees, as well as combined employer and employee contributions. These limitations include plan forfeitures.

Plan forfeitures are non-vested employer contributions that were made on behalf of participants, who are no longer employed by the company. We will review vesting on the next page.

The annual limits to contributions made into a 401(k) are the lesser of:

- 100 percent of the employee's compensation, or
- $53,000 (for 2016).
- The amount that employees can *contribute* under any 401(k) plan is limited to $18,000 for 2016. This amount normally increases with inflation, in $500 increments.

- 401(k) plans can allow *catch-up* contributions of $6,000 (for 2016) for any employee who is age 50 and over. This provision was created to allow older workers to save more than younger employees, as they have less time to see their investments grow.

Vesting:

All salary deferrals made by an employee are owned by that employee. Company contributions can be subject to a vesting schedule. Once a company contribution is vested, it is owned by the employee. Vesting is determined individually for each employee, and is based upon years of full-time service with the employer.

There is a maximum amount of time that can elapse before company contributions must become vested and owned by each individual employee. Vesting can occur gradually or all at once (cliff vesting). The following is the most restrictive, company-friendly vesting schedule allowed by law. This schedule can be found at the U.S. Department of Labor website:

http://www.dol.gov/ebsa/publications/401kplans.html

Graduated Vesting

Years of Service	Non-forfeitable Percentage
2	20%
3	40%
4	60%
5	80%
6	100%

Cliff Vesting

Less than 3 years of service - 0% Vested

At least 3 years of service - 100% Vested

Anti-Discrimination Rules

Retirement plans must treat all employees equally, and may not discriminate in favor of owners and top executives. The anti-discrimination rules govern how much employers can set aside for various employees, and how much employees can set aside for themselves.

Anti-discrimination rules limit the amount that can go into a plan for highly compensated employees (HCEs). This holds true for profit sharing contributions, as well as 401(k) deferrals.

HCE rules are complicated, and the percentages differ based upon a number of factors. The bottom line is this: Employers have limits on how much they can put into retirement plans for highly compensated executives. The same holds true with 401(k) deferrals. If highly compensated individuals defer too much, the plan must return contributions to bring deferral percentages into balance.

You can learn more about 401(k) testing requirements at the following IRS website:

http://www.irs.gov/retirement/article/0,,id=112858,00.html

What is an HCE?

An HCE is anyone who is a *5% owner* or is *highly compensated*, earning over $120,000 in 2016. In some cases, HCEs are anyone in the top 20% of company earners.

Note: There are several strategies that companies can use to allocate greater funds to owners and executives, without violating anti-discrimination rules. We will explore these soon.

Safe Harbor 401(k)

A safe harbor 401(k) allows HCEs to contribute the maximum, regardless of how much non-HCEs defer. It also reduces plan recordkeeping costs.

A plan can qualify for safe harbor treatment in two ways:

1. The employer can make a fully-vested, non-elective contribution of 3 percent (of each eligible employee's compensation) into the plan.

2. The employer can agree to match every eligible employee's *contributions* into the plan. This match must be dollar for dollar, of up to 3 percent of each employee's compensation. The employer can choose to match an additional 50 cents on every dollar up to 5 percent of each employee's contribution. This brings the total maximum match to 4%.

To remain under the safe harbor provisions, employers must make either the matching contributions or the non-elective contributions every year.

The sponsor's plan document must specify which contributions will be made. This information must be provided to all eligible employees before the beginning of each year.

Chapter Eight

_____R_____

Integrated Plans

Integrated Plans

Retirement plan contributions can be "integrated" with Social Security.

Integration is based upon the concept that Social Security provides retirement benefits to all employees, but not all income. In 2016, the Social Security maximum taxable wage base is $118,500. Social Security ignores all income above the taxable wage base, and will not pay benefits upon that income.

With integrated contributions, employees earning less than the Social Security wage base receive a pro rata allocation into the retirement plan, based upon compensation. Those earning above the taxable wage base are eligible to receive an additional contribution, potentially as much as 5.7% of the excess compensation over the wage base.

The reason that integration is allowed is simple: Social Security does not pay benefits to retirees on earnings above the taxable wage base. To make up for this disparity, employers are allowed to make additional contributions into a plan under an integrated profit sharing formula.

Integration can be used to legally increase contributions to executives, as a method to make *total* retirement benefits, including Social Security, more equal for employees.

Chapter Nine

R

Age Weighted Profit Sharing Plans

Age Weighted Profit Sharing Plans

Businesses can make use of a concept called "age weighting" with their profit sharing contributions.

In certain situations, age weighting allows far greater contributions to be made for a select group of older employees.

Equality is Deductible

One of the primary components of ERISA legislation was to limit the deductibility of company contributions into retirement plans. A main intent of the law was to create "equality" with regard to company contributions.

Entrepreneurial Rewards

Most small and mid-sized companies are privately held, and owned by one or a few individuals. Many successful entrepreneurs took enormous risks with their personal finances, and sacrificed for many years before achieving their current financial success. These business owners pay competitive wages. They pay employees *before* they pay themselves. Many still endure sleepless nights wondering how to remain competitive.

Once a business owner achieves financial success, the IRS demands a significant portion of profits for *taxes*.

High taxes create an incentive for business owners, and executives to put as much into their retirement plans as possible.

Traditional profit sharing formulas don't allow employers to allocate a high percentage of company contributions to the ownership/executive group. Under standard profit sharing, the executive group will receive the same percentage that is given to all other employees. Or less, because of contribution limits.

Age Weighting: Equal More Than "Equal"

Congress realized that equality does not always mean allocating the same *percentage* contribution into a plan for all employees. Equality can also mean making contributions to achieve the same *benefit* at retirement.

This concession by Congress creates planning opportunities for certain businesses.

With age weighting, companies are often able to make profit sharing contributions that allocate a significant portion of contributions to the older *management group*. With this technique it is not unusual for owner/executives to receive *50% - 90% of company contributions*.

Age Weighting

Traditional profit sharing contributions are made as a percentage of employee compensation. If the company decides upon a 10% contribution, everybody in the plan gets treated the same, with 10% of pay.

With age weighting, employees are also treated equally. In this case, "equal" may mean that one employee (someone young) receives a 1% contribution, while another (the older owner/executive) receives 25%. This is because age weighting adds a *future value* feature to the "equality" equation.

Equal Future Value

- For a plan to obtain favorable tax treatment there must be no discrimination against employees.

- Congress recognized that a similar percentage contribution to all employees can inadvertently *discriminate* against *older* employees. This is because older employees have less time to see their investments grow before retirement.

Focus on the *Future* Benefit

An employee's age relates directly to how long plan contributions can grow before retirement. For example: A $5,000 contribution might grow little in one year. With 8% annual growth, this same $5,000 would grow to more than $50,000 in thirty years.

Plan trustees (and their administrators) can use this time value to tweak profit sharing contributions in favor of older employees.

Note: From 1928 to 2014, the arithmetic average annual rate of return for S&P 500 was 11.53%. Ten-year U.S. Treasury Bonds returned an average of 5.28%. While there is no guarantee that we will see the same returns over the next 85 years, prudent managers keep long-term averages in mind as they plan.

Source:http://pages.stern.nyu.edu/~adamodar/New_Home_Page/datafile/histretSP.html

The decade from 1998-2008 was challenging for retirement plan investors. The returns for both stocks and bonds were below their long-term averages. Over time, stock and bond returns revert to long-term averages that vary less and less as time horizons expand.

Current interest rates are unusually low. This is due to the stimulative monetary policies of the Federal Reserve. The Federal Funds Rate has been kept near zero for almost a decade. This is unprecedented in modern financial times, and has led to poor bond returns. Low interest rates should not remain low forever; at least they never have. But they will continue to punish low-risk savers until they gravitate back toward their historical norms.

How Age-weighting Works

With age-weighting, administrators assume a rate of return on investments from the contribution date until retirement. This rate of return must be within legal guidelines that are established by law. Contribution are made for each employee, to give them all the *same percentage (of pay) benefit at retirement* — not the same percentage of today's compensation.

In our simplified example from above, a $5,000 contribution for someone thirty years from retirement (age 35) is essentially the *same* as a $50,000 contribution made for an employee retiring in a year (age 64).

Another Example:

Let's compare the contributions for an employee who is age twenty-five versus contributions made for an employee who is age fifty-five. Our twenty-five-year-old will have forty years (assuming retirement at age 65) to grow a 10% profit sharing contribution, while an employee who is fifty-five will have only ten years.

If we assume an investment rate of return of 7.2%, our young employee will see this year's 10% plan contribution grow to

160% of current salary in forty years. Our older employee will see his/her 10% grow in the plan to just 20% of current salary in ten years. This is a factor of 8:1.

With age-weighting, to get the same 160% of current pay at retirement, our older employee would need to receive a profit sharing contribution of **80%** to receive the same *equal benefit as* a **10%** contribution for the younger employee. This is the same factor of 8:1. Conversely, the younger employee may receive a contribution of *1.25%* **versus** *10%* to receive *equal benefit* under the plan. This maintains the same factor of 8:1.

Example: The following illustrates the benefit of age weighting in retirement plan design:

Assume we have a small tech company, with an owner who is age 55 and two high-income employees who are age 25. Our owner earns $100,000. Each of our younger employees earn $100,000 as well. This gives us a total payroll of $300,000.

Under the traditional profit sharing concept, a 10% profit sharing contribution would lead to a total deposit into the plan of $30,000. One third goes to benefit the owner (10% of $100,000). Two thirds benefits the employees (10% of $100,000 each).

Our owner now needs to make a choice. Should she make the profit sharing contribution? Let's do the math.

Assuming a 30% total owner tax bracket, our owner would keep $21,000, after paying taxes on the $30,000 of profit.

Contributions into a profit sharing plan are tax deductible. In this example, our owner would pay no income taxes if she contributes the $30,000 into a profit sharing plan. If she makes this contribution, our owner would have $10,000 in her own account, rather than $21,000, after taxes, if she had just kept the money and paid the tax.

In this simplified example, our owner is $11,000 out-of-pocket if she contributes $30,000 to the profit sharing plan. Our owner will be tempted to keep her personal money and forget about funding the plan.

With age weighting, our owner would be able to make the same $30,000 contribution. In this case, $26,175 would be contributed to the owner's account. $1,875 would be set aside for each employee. If the employees earn less than the owner, smaller contributions would be made to their accounts.

With age-weighting, our business owner will be more inclined to make a profit sharing contribution. Everybody wins. Our owner is happy because she has saved more for retirement. The employees are happy, because they have received a profit sharing contribution. The taxing authorities will receive $9,000 less in current owner income taxes.

Age-weighting can be a very attractive profit sharing feature for a business with older executives.

Note: Calculations for age weighted plans are not quite so simple. Adjustments must be made for owners and highly compensated employees. There are limits to how much can be set aside for any single individual. Employees might be segregated into groups for other testing reasons, etc. Age weighted contributions can be made in different ways. A good explanation of actuarial calculations can be found here:

http://www.actuaries.org/LIBRARY/ASTIN/vol33no2/289.pdf

Talk to your advisors if you think age-weighting could be of benefit to your company.

Chapter Ten

R

New Comparability/Cross Tested

New Comparability/Cross-Tested Plans

All businesses face financial challenges. Regulation is costly. Competition is fierce. Some companies compete against foreign operators with far less regulation and lower salary scales.

Private business owners and executives would like to set aside tax-favored funds while they can. This money can be used in retirement. It is also unavailable to creditors in the event of a business failure.

In a perfect world, management groups would set aside as much as possible into retirement accounts for all employees. Reality makes this a challenge. Every dollar matters.

Employers must weigh making retirement plan contributions against many other options. Can extra funds be used for company expansion? Can they be used to hire new employees? Should they be used to increase pay for key individuals, or should they be set aside to weather future economic downturns? Should ownership take the money, pay the taxes and keep the balance?

A Magnificent Option

Cross-testing is a hybrid plan design that can be used to direct a *much higher percentage* of employer contributions to the *management/owner group.* It uses the concept of age-weighting, but with creative twists that can create even more benefit for executives.

Comparability designs can create a win-win for employers *and* employees. Executive/owners are able to set aside a significant portion of contributions for themselves. Employees benefit from contributions they would not otherwise receive.

How It Works

Cross-tested plans allow the employer (trustees) to place eligible participants into various "tiers." Contributions are made on an *age-weighted* basis, using all employees within tiers for calculations, rather than each particular individual.

Tiers can be created based upon a variety of factors, such as, but not limited to:

- Company Position.
- Compensation.
- Longevity on the Job.
- Sales or Management Goals.

Plan sponsors are also allowed to use a combination of traditional tier factors to create a *unique* tier that suits the company.

Individuals within each tier can receive differing amounts, yet still be treated "equally" under the law.

Why Create Tiers?

Tiers can be used to bring contributions within acceptable limits to avoid discrimination. By using tiers, businesses can create enormous flexibility with regard to retirement plan benefits and contributions. For example: If one individual in a tier opts to receive nothing, others may take the remaining allocation. **This allows certain employees to receive far larger contributions than under traditional plan designs.**

Here is a simple example of how it might work:

Let's say that contributions into a particular tier can average no more than 10%. We create a tier that has two members — the chairman of the board and his child, the CEO. Our chairman is semi-retired and has no need for retirement plan contributions. We set aside zero for our chairman. This allows us to set aside 20% for our CEO (averaging 10% for the tier) and avoid discrimination.

Here is another use:

A business owner is trying to recruit a new CEO from outside the company. By electing a zero contribution, our business owner is able to set aside 20% for the new CEO, creating a powerful (yet legal) tax-deductible perk to entice the new executive.

There are dozens of favorable ways that comparability can be used to tailor contributions into retirement plans.

$&¢

Chapter Eleven

_____R_____

Plan Design: A Comparative Example

PLAN DESIGN: A COMPARATIVE EXAMPLE

The following is an example of how contributions can vary between three different plan designs.

The original design featured an age-weighted profit sharing plan.

The second plan design included an integrated formula to allow for greater contributions for the ownership team. Contributions for ownership increase by $11,000. Unfortunately, it also increases total company contributions by nearly $30,000.

The third plan utilized an age-weighted comparability design. This design allowed the employer to fund the *same* amount for ownership as the original design. It also allowed the company to ***reduce total contributions into the plan by $130,000.***

The following pages illustrate the real-life calculations. Ownership is represented in Group 1:

ABC, INC. Pension Plan
Pension Plan Specifications
20xx Plan Year

Effective Date: 1/1/xxxx
Valuation Date: 12/31/xxxx

Eligibility:

Minimum Age	21
Minimum Service	None
Entry Date	First day of the month following hire.
Normal Retirement Age:	65

ABC, INC. Pension Plan
Total Contribution:
Current Integrated Plan
$296,167, based on applying current Money Purchase Formula to total.

Alternative Integrated Plan
$324,864, based on increasing excess percentage over Taxable Wage Base from 2.8% to 5.7%.

Comparability Plan
$165,494, based on giving Group 1 members the same dollar contribution as they would receive under the Current Integrated Plan. Contributions for other groups were arbitrarily chosen and can be easily changed.

Notes:
Under Comparability Plan:
Group 1 A,B,C,D
Group 2 E,F
Group 3 Others
Compensation used is total pay, including bonuses.

SUMMARY OF RETIREMENT PROGRAMS

ABC, INC. Pension Plan

For the Period   1/1/xxxx through 12/31/xxxx

Profit Sharing Contribution

Name	Age	Total Plan Comp	Current Comparability Plan	Alternative Integrated Plan	Integrated Plan
Group 1					
A	51	170,000	19,626	19,626	22,347
B	41	170,000	19,626	19,626	22,347
C	47	170,000	19,626	19,626	22,347
D	42	170,000	19,626	19,626	22,347
Total Group 1		680,000	78,504	78,504	89,388
Group 2					
E	32	170,000	10,200	19,626	22,347
F	47	170,000	10,200	19,626	22,347
Total Group 2		340,000	20,400	39,252	44,694
Group 3					
G	52	43,000	1,720	4,300	4,300
H	23	35,000	1,400	3,500	3,500
I	28	50,000	2,000	5,000	5,000
J	28	115,000	4,600	12,586	13,712
K	24	60,000	2,400	6,000	6,000
L	32	80,000	3,200	8,106	8,217
M	32	164,000	6,560	18,858	21,405
N	27	37,080	1,483	3,708	3,708
O	36	152,000	6,080	17,322	19,521

P	38	18,500	740	1,850	1,850
Q	28	52,000	2,080	5,200	5,200
R	56	85,104	3,404	8,760	9,018
S	48	75,833	3,033	7,583	7,583
T	41	170,000	6,800	19,626	22,347
U	35	113,000	4,520	12,330	13,398
V	29	65,000	2,600	6,500	6,500
W	24	40,000	1,600	4,000	4,000
X	42	79,250	3,170	8,010	8,099
Y	34	130,000	5,200	14,506	16,067
Z	37	100,000	4,000	10,666	11,357
Total Group 3		1,664,768	66,590	178,411	190,782
TOTAL		2,684,768	165,494	296,167	324,86

** This illustration is based on the assumption that each listed participant receives a contribution. If this is not the case, then the actual allocation of the total contribution may differ.

TOTAL: $2,684,768 Compensation

Comparability	Current Integrated	Alternate Integrated
$165,494	$296,167	$324,864

SUMMARY OF RETIREMENT PROGRAMS
ABC, INC. Pension Plan

For the Period   1/1/xxxx through 12/31/xxxx

Profit Sharing Contribution as % Pay

Name	Age	Total Comp	Current Comparability Plan	Alternative Integrated Plan	Integrated Plan
Group 1					
A	51	170,000	11.54%	11.54%	13.15%
B	41	170,000	11.54%	11.54%	13.15%
C	47	170,000	11.54%	11.54%	13.15%
D	42	170,000	11.54%	11.54%	13.15%
Total Group 1		680,000	11.54%	11.54%	13.15%
Group 2					
E	32	170,000	6.00%	11.54%	13.15%
F	47	170,000	6.00%	11.54%	13.15%
Total Group 2		340,000	6.00%	11.54%	13.15%
Group 3					
G	52	43,000	4.00%	10.00%	10.00%
H	23	35,000	4.00%	10.00%	10.00%
I	28	50,000	4.00%	10.00%	10.00%
J	28	115,000	4.00%	10.94%	11.92%
K	24	60,000	4.00%	10.00%	10.00%
L	32	80,000	4.00%	10.13%	10.27%
M	32	164,000	4.00%	11.50%	13.05%
N	27	37,080	4.00%	10.00%	10.00%

O	36	152,000	4.00%	11.40%	12.84%
P	38	18,500	4.00%	10.00%	10.00%
Q	28	52,000	4.00%	10.00%	10.00%
R	56	85,104	4.00%	10.29%	10.60%
S	48	75,833	4.00%	10.00%	10.00%
T	41	170,000	4.00%	11.54%	13.15%
U	35	113,000	4.00%	10.91%	11.86%
V	29	65,000	4.00%	10.00%	10.00%
W	24	40,000	4.00%	10.00%	10.00%
X	42	79,250	4.00%	10.11%	10.22%
Y	34	130,000	4.00%	11.16%	12.36%
Z	37	100,000	4.00%	10.67%	11.36%
Total Group 3		1,664,768	4.00%	10.72%	11.46%
TOTAL		2,684,768	6.16%	11.03%	12.10%

** This illustration is based on the assumption that each listed participant receives a contribution. If this is not the case, then the actual allocation of the total contribution may differ.

TOTAL: $2,684,768 Compensation

Comparability	Current Integrated	Alternate Integrated
$165,494	$296,167	$324,864

SUMMARY OF RETIREMENT PROGRAMS
ABC, INC. Pension Plan

For the Period   1/1/20xx through 12/31/20xx

Profit Sharing Contribution as % Pay

Name	Age	Total Comp	Current Comparability Plan	Alternative Integrated Plan	Integrated Plan
Group 1					
A	51	170,000	11.54%	11.54%	13.15%
B	41	170,000	11.54%	11.54%	13.15%
C	47	170,000	11.54%	11.54%	13.15%
D	42	170,000	11.54%	11.54%	13.15%
Total Group 1		680,000	11.54%	11.54%	13.15%
Group 2					
E	32	170,000	6.00%	11.54%	13.15%
F	47	170,000	6.00%	11.54%	13.15%
Total Group 2		340,000	6.00%	11.54%	13.15%
Group 3					
G	52	43,000	4.00%	10.00%	10.00%
H	23	35,000	4.00%	10.00%	10.00%
I	28	50,000	4.00%	10.00%	10.00%
J	28	115,000	4.00%	10.94%	11.92%
K	24	60,000	4.00%	10.00%	10.00%
L	32	80,000	4.00%	10.13%	10.27%
M	32	164,000	4.00%	11.50%	13.05%
N	27	37,080	4.00%	10.00%	10.00%

O	36	152,000	4.00%	11.40%	12.84%
P	38	18,500	4.00%	10.00%	10.00%
Q	28	52,000	4.00%	10.00%	10.00%
R	56	85,104	4.00%	10.29%	10.60%
S	48	75,833	4.00%	10.00%	10.00%
T	41	170,000	4.00%	11.54%	13.15%
U	35	113,000	4.00%	10.91%	11.86%
V	29	65,000	4.00%	10.00%	10.00%
W	24	40,000	4.00%	10.00%	10.00%
X	42	79,250	4.00%	10.11%	10.22%
Y	34	130,000	4.00%	11.16%	12.36%
Z	37	100,000	4.00%	10.67%	11.36%
Total Group 3		1,664,768	4.00%	10.72%	11.46%
TOTAL		2,684,768	6.16%	11.03%	12.10%

	Comparability	Age Weighted	Integrated
Group 1	$78,504	$78,504	$89,388
Group 2	$20,400	$39,252	$44,694
Group 3	$66,590	$178,411	$190,782

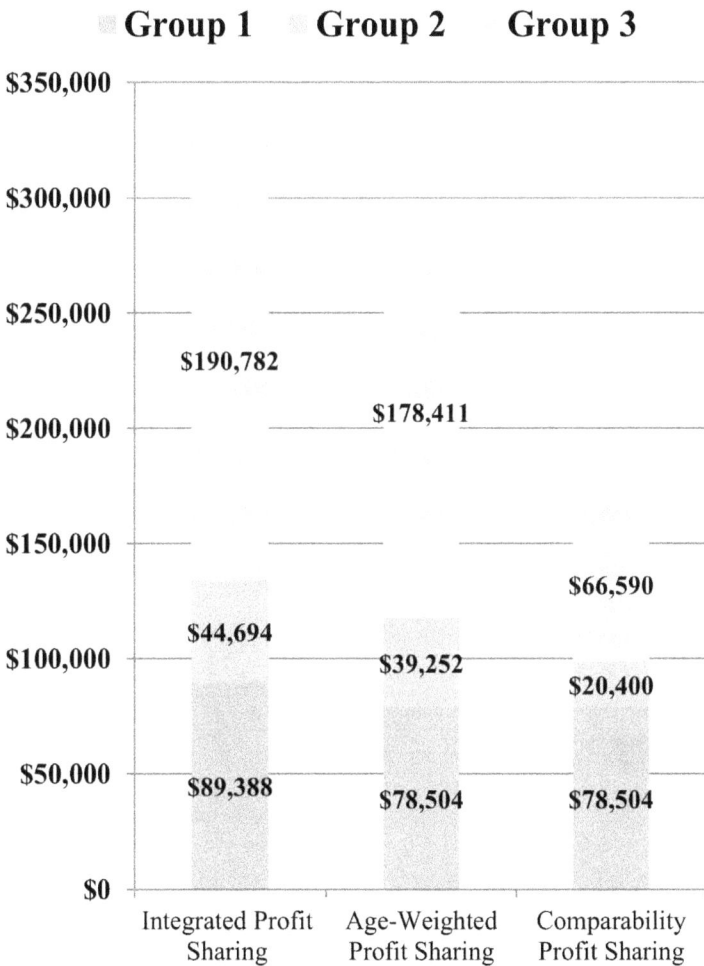

Group 1   Group 2   Group 3

Integrated Profit Sharing: Group 1 $89,388, Group 2 $44,694, Group 3 $190,782

Age-Weighted Profit Sharing: Group 1 $78,504, Group 2 $39,252, Group 3 $178,411

Comparability Profit Sharing: Group 1 $78,504, Group 2 $20,400, Group 3 $66,590

$&C

Chapter Twelve

R
_____

Defined Benefit Pensions for Private Business

Defined Benefit Pensions for Private Business

Defined benefit (DB) pension plans can be unusually attractive to smaller businesses, particularly those with older executives and owners.

In certain circumstances, DB plans can set aside 100% (or more) of an executive's pay into a plan each year. Contributions are tax deductible and grow tax deferred. The money is not accessible by creditors.

Here is a simple example:

Let's say that we have a business owner/executive who is age 55. She wants to retire at age 65. The owner takes a salary of $100,000 for living expenses. She is earning an additional $200,000 per year, all of it taxable.

We establish a pension plan that will pay our owner/exec 100% of salary at age 65. This gives us ten years to accumulate sufficient assets in the plan to pay our exec $100,000 per year for life.

Our actuaries run calculations. The calculations tell us that we will need $1,500,000 in ten years to provide our planned retirement benefit. How much must we set aside each year to achieve our $1.5 million?

With a zero rate of return, we would need to contribute $150,000 per year. Assuming a 6% return, an annual deposit of $110,000 would approach $1.5 million in ten years. Our sample executive is able to put $110,000 into the plan in year one.

The current maximum allowable retirement benefit is $210,000. In this case, by increasing her salary closer to $150,000, our owner could deposit her remaining $150,000 income into the plan. With a 30% tax bracket, our business owner will reduce her personal taxes by about $50,000 per year.

Each year, our actuary will value the plan assets. The actuary will calculate the asset value against an assumed future rate of return and life expectancy. This will determine our deposits in later years. If we earn less than our expected 6%, we can put more into the plan. If we earn more, our future deposits may be less. If salary decreases, so might contributions.

If our business owner has employees, deposits must be made for them as well. If these employees leave the company, they will be due the "present value of any (vested) future benefits." As we discussed in a prior chapter, this may be a relatively small sum, especially if the employees are young.

Summary

With any small, consistently profitable company, a defined benefit pension plan can be highly attractive as a way to set aside large sums of money in a tax-friendly manner.

Professionals like physicians, CPAs and law firms have been known to use this technique as a way to buy out senior management.

Aging owners have used it as a way to transition out of a business in favor of the next generation.

Businesses use it as a recruiting tool to attract skilled senior management from outside the company.

Could this be a winning strategy for your company?

$&¢

Chapter Thirteen

R

412(i) Plans

412(i)

A 412(i) is a defined pension plan that uses only life insurance and annuity contracts as the investment vehicle(s). A 412(i) allows for *much higher* contributions than traditional defined benefit plans. This is because actuaries are allowed to assume a very low rate of return on investments, until and during retirement.

A 412(i) can be attractive for individuals who want *high deductions* and *low risk* investments for the plan. It is also attractive for individuals seeking assets that cannot be attached by creditors.

While a well-designed 412(i) is perfectly legal, care must be taken that this type of plan is the appropriate choice, and structured properly. 412(i) plans have been abused by a few insurance agents seeking high commissions. Designs that utilize life insurance as the only investment vehicle run counter to the original intent of IRS approval.

You should ask many questions and seek informed counsel before entering into this type of arrangement. If appropriate and structured properly, a 412(i) plan may be an attractive choice for a small, consistently profitable business.

$&¢

Chapter Fourteen

_____R_____

ESOPs

ESOPs

An Employee Stock Ownership Plan (ESOP) is a form of qualified plan that can be appropriate in certain situations. While many business executives are not aware of ESOPs, they benefit more than 11 million workers in the United States.

ESOPs are extremely useful and flexible, but complicated. ESOPs can be used to:

- Purchase stock from company owners. If structured properly, sales proceeds may be tax free.
- Provide incentive for employees to maintain profitability.
- Retire company debt in a tax deductible manner.
- Give (most) benefits of corporate ownership to employees while maintaining voting control of the shares.
- Improve current cash flow.

How It Works:

An ESOP is similar to a profit sharing plan, except that the ESOP invests in company stock, rather than other investments. All eligible employees must be part of the plan. The plan can have a vesting schedule. Vesting will either a three-year "cliff," or 20% per year.

Company stock can go into the plan in several ways:

- The company may contribute treasury stock into the plan, in the same manner as cash into a profit sharing plan. Contributions are tax deductible to the company.

- The company may contribute cash, which is used to purchase stock from current owners.

- The plan may borrow money (typically from a bank), to make a single, larger purchase of stock from owners or the company.

    o This can be used to "cash out" an owner, often with little taxation.

    o The company then makes *deductible* cash contributions to the plan, which retire the bank debt over time.

A good resource for understanding ESOPs is the National Center for Employee Ownership, which can be found at:

http://www.nceo.org.

Chapter Fifteen

R

Solo 401(K) Plans

Solo 401(k)

An Individual 401(k) works like a traditional 401(k), except that it is for owners, partners, and their spouses only. There can be no other employees.

The plan can utilize pre-tax contributions, like a traditional 401(k). It can also be structured as a Roth 401(k), where contributions are made on an after-tax basis, but come out tax-free.

Solo 401(k)s are an ideal choice for professionals, such as doctors, writers, lawyers, consultants, accountants, tradesmen, and programmers.

In today's shifting workplace, many people are becoming independent contractors. This type of retirement plan works well for individuals who don't work as traditional employees, but for themselves.

Here are the general rules for a Solo 401(k):

- Employer/owners may contribute up to $53,000, depending on their compensation, by making a combination of the following:

- o Salary deferrals of up to $18,500. This cannot exceed 100% of compensation.
- o Company contributions of up to 25% of compensation (or up to 20% of self-employment income).

- Catch-up contributions, of up to $6,000, can be made annually for individuals over age 50, to a maximum total contribution of $59,000.

- Contributions can be made in the traditional, tax deductible 401(k) manner. Medicare and Social Security taxes must still be paid.

- Contributions can also be made with after-tax contributions by using a Roth feature.

  - o A Roth 401(k) can ultimately be rolled into a Roth IRA.

- Other retirement plan assets can usually be rolled into a Solo 401(k) plan. Rollovers can be made from a SEP, SARSEP, SIMPLE IRA (after two years), traditional IRA, rollover IRA, Keogh, 401(k), 403(b) and 457 plans.

- Loans are allowable from most Solo 401(k) plans. This varies, according to the administrator of the plan.

- Withdrawals before the age of 591/2 are subject to a 10% penalty tax. This tax is in addition to normal income taxation on the withdrawal.

If your company is eligible for an Individual 401(k), you should take advantage. Solo 401(k)s are a low-cost, simple way to accumulate assets in a tax-favored manner.

Chapter Sixteen

R

Stock Bonus Plans

STOCK BONUS PLANS

A stock bonus plan is a qualified plan that allows for employer stock to be contributed to the plan in lieu of cash. They are used by employers as an employee retirement vehicle, and a productivity tool.

With stock bonus plans, employees gain a personal interest in the financial fortunes of a company. Employees will work harder to see that profits increase, since an increase in profit translates to a rise in stock value.

Stock bonus plans can also help employers *increase* current cash flow. When treasury stock is contributed to a qualified plan, the value of stock contributions is a tax deductible expense to the company — even if the stock is privately held. This reduces taxable profits. This results in lower taxation and preserves company cash.

A traditional profit sharing or 401(k) plan can receive employer stock as company contributions. Company stock can also be offered as an investment option. Large, public companies often contribute company stock for their 401(k) matching contributions.

Contributions to a stock bonus plan are generally discretionary, and made on a year-by-year basis, just as traditional profit sharing payments. The same holds true when used as a 401(k) match. Companies often guarantee matching contributions at the beginning of each year, but rarely extend guarantees into future years.

Earnings in a stock bonus plan accrue on a tax-deferred basis, as in any qualified plan. Contributions and earnings become taxable to participants when they are withdrawn from their stock bonus account.

When distributions are made from a stock bonus plan, participants must have the right to demand that their employer stock be distributed from the plan. If employer securities are not publicly traded, employees must also be given the right to receive cash for their shares, based upon a *fair value formula*. This value must be determined by an independent, valuation professional.

If employer shares are distributed, employees must be allowed to sell stock back to the employer for a period of 60 days. This is known as a "put" option. The employer must also open a 60 day purchase window at the end of each plan year. This window is available to holders who did not exercise their 60-day put option during the plan year.

Summary:

A stock bonus plan can be a valuable tool in the retirement plan toolbox. Stock bonuses give employees a powerful incentive to see that a company is profitable. Bonus plans can be implemented with a relatively small initial outlay. Care must be taken to manage future costs, particularly when employees begin to leave and demand cash. Regular company valuations must be conducted, and made available to employees, which may or may not be a privacy issue with ownership.

Chapter Seventeen

R

457 Plans

457 Plans

Most state and local governments, as well as some non-governmental entities, are tax exempt under Section 501 of the Internal Revenue Code. This means that they pay no income taxes. These "non-profit" entities are allowed to establish tax-favored, *deferred compensation plans* for their employees under Section 457 of the Internal Revenue Code.

The concept of deferred compensation is somewhat similar to that of a 401(k).

- Employees elect to defer a portion of their pay.

- Employees are not taxed on deferrals.

- Deferrals grow tax free.

- The benefits are taxed as income, when received by the employee.

- The employer may offer several different forms of investment choices.

- Employee deferrals may be placed into a pool, where they earn a common rate of return with all other deferrals.

- Deferrals may be placed into separate accounts, even placed into mutual funds, where they are directed by the employee.

  o In this arrangement, employees earn the net return of their investment portfolio.

- The employer may or may not choose to match deferrals.

In traditional deferred compensation, employee deferrals are retained as assets of the employer, and are offset by a liability to the employee. In the event of a default by the employer, employees can lose their deferrals to other creditors with more seniority. In governmental plans, the risk of default is normally lower, due to their taxing authority.

With the advent of separate accounts, an employee may have little or no chance of losing funds.

- Under current (2016) law, employees in a 457 Plan are able to defer a maximum of $18,000.

- **Special Note:** In many cases, teachers are allowed to participate in a 457 Plan *and* a 403(b) Plan concurrently. This includes catch-up contributions for both plans.

Chapter Eighteen

R

403(b) Plans

403(b) Plans

A 403(b) Plan is a retirement plan for certain employees of public schools, tax-exempt organizations and ministers.

Like a 401(k), employees can elect to defer a portion of their income into the plan. Employers can make non-elective contributions. There can be a combination of deferrals and company contributions.

Contributions into a 403(b) can also be made on an after-tax basis.

For many years, 403(b) retirement plans were required (by law) to be in the form of an annuity. They became known as "tax-sheltered annuities," or TSA plans.

In 2007, the 403(b) rules became very similar to those of 401(k) plans, particularly with regard to *fiduciary* responsibility. Many schools and charitable non-profits are now allowed to adopt 401(k)s in lieu of their 403(b)s.

Like a 401(k), employee deferrals are not subject to current federal income taxes. Most states do not tax deferrals, but a few still do. Contributors must still pay Social Security and Medicare taxes.

Annual contribution limits are the same as with a 401(k) plan.

403(b)s do have a significant advantage over 401(k)s: There is no ADP (average deferral percentage) testing for non-ERISA 403(b) plans. Highly compensated executive (HCE) deferrals are not limited by the average deferral percentage of non-HCEs. Each HCE can defer the maximum, regardless of how much non-HCEs contribute to the plan.

Like a 401(k), 403(b) deferrals go into individual accounts for employees. Deferrals can be deposited into any of the following types of entities:

- An annuity contract. This is a contract provided through an insurance company.

- A custodial account. These are usually invested in mutual funds.

- A retirement income account set up for church employees. This type of account will normally invest in annuities or mutual funds.

Chapter Nineteen

R

Roth 401(k) Plans

Roth 401(k)

A Roth 401(k) combines the features of a traditional 401(k) with those of a Roth IRA. The primary difference between a traditional 401(k) and a Roth 401(k) is when monies are taxed.

With the traditional 401(k) monies are:

- Tax deductible when contributed. (Some states may still tax deferrals.)
- Tax deferred as they grow.
- Taxed when removed from the plan or a subsequent IRA.

With a Roth 401(k) monies are:

- Not tax deductible when contributed. All contributions are subject to normal income taxes in the year of deposit.
- Tax deferred as they grow.

- Tax free when removed from the plan or a subsequent Roth IRA. (Subject to certain limitations.)

The Roth retirement plan provisions were enacted as part of the Economic Growth and Tax Relief Reconciliation Act of 2001 (EGTRRA). Beginning in 2006, employers were allowed to amend existing 401(k) documents to allow employees to elect Roth IRA treatment of a portion or all of their 401(k) contributions.

Employers are allowed to make matching contributions to an employee's Roth contributions. However, employer contributions are treated in the same manner as traditional 401(k) matching contributions. They must be segregated into a *pre-tax* account.

Who Wants a Roth?

- Roth IRA contributions can be advantageous for younger workers who are in a low tax bracket today, but expect to earn more in the future. Paying a little tax today could save significant taxes in the future, as assets compound in growth.

- A Roth can also be attractive to wealthy individuals who want to leave a *tax-free* legacy for their heirs.

Roth 403(b)

- A Roth 403(b) has the same characteristics as a traditional 403(b), but with the unique Roth tax provisions.

Chapter Twenty

_____R_____

IRAs

IRAs

IRAs are individual retirement arrangements. IRAs were created so that individuals could have the same retirement advantages as employees covered under company qualified plans.

The major features of IRAs are as follows:

- An IRA is an Individual Retirement Arrangement/Ac-
  count.

- IRAs are always owned and controlled by the individual, not by an employer.

- IRAs can be formed and funded by individuals for
  themselves.

- IRAs can also be part of an employer-sponsored retirement plan and funded by employers.

In most cases, individuals are able to take a tax deduction for
funds that are contributed to an IRA. Contributions grow tax-
deferred. They are taxed when they are withdrawn from the

account.

As with anything having to do with favorable tax treatment, there are rules and regulations regarding deductibility for income tax purposes. There may also be tax penalties for removing money before a certain age (59 1/2), or for not taking minimum distributions after a certain age (70 1/2).

This book does not go into great depth regarding IRAs. Our focus is on how IRAs interface with qualified plans provided by employers.

Deductibility

The deductibility of IRA deposits is affected by whether or not an employee is *participating* in a company-sponsored plan. Deductibility is also affected by a taxpayer's *adjusted gross income* for tax purposes. Adjusted gross income is the amount of income used by the IRS to determine tax liability.

Destination

Most of the money that is held inside qualified retirement plans will eventually find its way into an individual IRA. This normally happens when an employee terminates service with a company. When an employee leaves a company, they will have the option to transfer their retirement funds from a qualified plan to an IRA. This is done with a transaction called a "trustee to trustee" transfer.

By moving the funds from a qualified vehicle to an IRA, employees can avoid the immediate taxation of all benefit proceeds.

A Brief IRA History

Because IRAs are a retirement tool that is constantly changing, it will be helpful to review their legislative history.

IRAs were created with the enactment of the Employee Retirement Income Security Act (ERISA), in 1974.

Initially, individuals were allowed to contribute up to $1,500 per year into an IRA, provided they were not covered by qualified retirement plan.

The Economic Recovery Tax Act of 1981 (ERTA) expanded the use of IRAs. This act removed the qualified plan restriction, allowing all taxpayers (under the age of 70½) to contribute to IRAs. ERTA raised the maximum annual contribution to $2,000, and allowed participants to contribute $250 for a nonworking spouse. At that time, all IRA contributions were tax deductible, and were taxable when withdrawn.

The Tax Reform Act of 1986 created deduction phase out provisions for IRA contributions made by high-earning employees (or their spouses) that were covered by employment-based retirement plans.

The Small Business Job Protection Act of 1996 raised the limit for contributions on behalf of nonworking spouses from $250 to $2,000.

The Taxpayer Relief Act of 1997 created the *Roth IRA*.

- Roth IRA contributions are not deductible for income tax purposes.
- The growth of Roth IRA assets is tax free.
- Withdrawals from a Roth IRA are tax free.

Besides creating the Roth, the Taxpayer Relief Act of 1997 made other significant changes to IRAs. The act increased the income threshold, above which deductible contributions were phased out. It also made adjustments to the eligibility of tax-payers who were covered (and whose spouses were covered) by an employment-based plan.

The Economic Growth and Tax Relief Reconciliation Act of 2001 raised the limit on contributions beginning in 2002. It also allowed for catch-up contributions to be made by people age 50 and above. The provisions of this act, (as well those of the Jobs and Growth Tax Relief Reconciliation Act of 2003) were extended until 2012.

The American Taxpayer Relief Act of 2012 gave permanency to many of the EGTRRA changes. It lifted many of the restrictions on Roth conversions within 401(k) plans. It also allowed individuals to make tax-free charitable contributions from an IRA, of up to $100,000 per year.

EVER CHANGING

Congress has made many changes to IRAs over the years, and will continue to do so. Some of your employees will have personal or rollover IRAs. Others will have them when they retire. It is a good idea for you to understand how they integrate with company sponsored plans, and how they add to employee financial security.

IRA DEDUCTIBILITY RULES

The deductibility of IRA contributions is affected by two factors:

- Participation (including spouses) in company-sponsored retirement plans.
- Adjusted gross income.

Complete details of the deductibility are available each year through IRS Publication 590:

https://www.irs.gov/publications/p590a/index.html

2016 Combined Traditional and Roth IRA Contribution Limits:

For someone under 50 years of age: The maximum contribution that can be made to a traditional or Roth IRA is the lesser of $5,500 or the amount of taxable compensation for 2016. This limit can be split between a traditional IRA and a Roth IRA. Regardless of the split, the combined limit is always $5,500. The maximum deductible contribution to a traditional IRA, and the maximum contribution to a Roth IRA, may be *reduced* depending on modified adjusted gross income. (See government tables.)

For someone 50 years of age or older: The maximum contribution that can be made to a traditional or Roth IRA is the smaller of $6,500 or the amount of taxable compensation for 2016. This limit can also be split between a traditional IRA and a Roth IRA. The combined limit is $6,500. The maximum deductible contribution to a traditional IRA and the maximum contribution to a Roth IRA may be *reduced* depending on modified adjusted gross income.

See government tables: http://www.irs.gov/pub/irs-pdf/p590.pdf

$&₵

Chapter Twenty-One

R
_____

Roth IRA Summary

ROTH IRA SUMMARY

The Taxpayer Relief Act of 1997 included a new twist to the IRA. Proposed by Senator William Roth of Delaware, a Roth IRA creates favorable tax treatment for when money is *withdrawn* from an IRA, *rather* than when it is placed into the plan.

Roth IRAs are most attractive to the wealthy, and younger savers who plan to have a high income when they retire.

Contributions to a Roth IRA are *not* tax deductible when made. However, contributions *grow tax free*, and are *not* subject to taxation when they are removed from the IRA.

Contributions can be made after the age of 70½, and individuals can leave assets in the IRA as long as they live. This feature can act as a useful estate planning tool — leaving assets to heirs that will escape income taxation forever.

Individuals are prohibited from contributing to Roth IRAs if their adjusted gross income is between and above certain levels. Higher limits exist for those who are married and filing jointly.

Certain individuals are allowed to convert a traditional IRA to a Roth IRA. However, they must pay current taxes, as if the money were fully distributed. The complete Roth IRA rules can be found here:

https://www.irs.gov/publications/p590a/index.html

ROTH 401(K) CONVERSIONS

Roth conversions are allowed from 401(k) assets under certain circumstances:

● First, the plan must allow for in-plan conversions. Not all plans do, nor are they required to offer this provision.

● Second, Roth conversions can only be made by eligible participants, normally employees who are terminating, or are over the age of 59 1/2.

The income limits for 401(k) Roth conversions were *eliminated* in 2010. This allows individuals with high incomes to establish Roth IRAs, and enjoy their unique tax benefits. Converting to a Roth is still a complicated endeavor, and should be managed under the supervision of competent counsel.

The IRS guide to Roth IRA and 401(k) conversions can be found at the following Internet location:

https://www.irs.gov/Retirement-Plans/Retirement-Plans-FAQs-regarding-IRAs-Rollovers-and-Roth-Conversions

Chapter Twenty-Two

R

SIMPLE IRA

SIMPLE IRA

A SIMPLE IRA (Savings Incentive Match Plan for Employees) can be established by businesses with less than 100 employees. This type of plan requires far less recordkeeping and administration than a traditional pension, profit sharing, or 401(k) plan.

Rather than contribute money into a centralized retirement plan, all company contributions, employee deferrals, and company matches are made into employee IRAs. The IRAs are controlled by each employee, not by the plan sponsor. They are typically housed with a single mutual fund company.

Salary reduction limits. The amount an employee may contribute to a SIMPLE IRA cannot exceed $12,500 in 2016.

If an employee participates in another employer plan during the year, the total amount of the salary reduction contributions the employee can make to all the plans is limited to $18,000 for 2016.

Catch-up contributions. If permitted by the SIMPLE IRA plan, participants who are age 50 or over, at the end of the calendar year, are allowed to make catch-up contributions. The catch-up contribution limit in 2016 is $3,000.

Simplified Administration

In order to qualify for the simplified recordkeeping and administration, a number of requirements must be met:

- The company must make a contribution of 2% of pay for all employees, or match employee deferrals dollar for dollar up to a minimum of 3% of pay.
  - o Company contributions are deductible.
- All company contributions must be 100% vested, immediately.
- Annual notices must be provided to all employees.
- Contributions and employee withholdings grow on a tax deferred basis.
- Funds will be taxed when they come out of the employee IRAs.

You can learn more about SIMPLE plans at the following location:

http://www.dol.gov/ebsa/publications/simple.html

Chapter Twenty-Three

_____R_____

Simplified Employee Pension Plans

SIMPLIFIED EMPLOYEE PENSIONS (SEPs)

A Simplified Employee Pension is available to any employer or sole proprietor. The primary advantage of a SEP is reduced administrative requirements and costs. Like in a SIMPLE plan, employer contributions are made to IRAs for the benefit of eligible employees. The primary features of a SEP are as follows:

- Discretionary contributions can be made up to 25% of pay, to a maximum of $53,000.

- Employees are not allowed to contribute to the plan.

- Vesting is immediate on 100% of plan contributions.

- Like any standard IRA, contributions grow on a tax deferred basis.

- Funds will be subject to taxation when removed from each individual's IRA.

More SEP information can be found here: https://www.irs.gov/Retirement-Plans/Plan-Sponsor/Simplified-Employee-Pension-Plan-(SEP)

A SARSEP is a simplified employee pension that allows for salary deferrals. SAREPs are no longer available to companies. Plans put in place prior to 1997 can remain in force. New hires must be allowed to participate. You can learn more about SARSEPs here:

http://www.irs.gov/retirement/article/0,,id=112859,00.html

Chapter Twenty-Four

R

The Department Of Labor
On Retirement Plans

THE DOL ON RETIREMENT PLANS:

A SUMMARY

If you are in charge of your company's retirement plan, you must ensure that you do things correctly. The Department of Labor is fussy when it comes to adhering to federal regulations. Below, you will find the DOL chart detailing the main characteristics of pension and profit sharing plans. Peruse this as a reference to how things can, and can't be done:

"Defined Benefit Plan   Defined Contribution Plan

Employer Contributions and/or Matching Contributions

Employer funded. Federal rules set amounts that employers must contribute to plans in an effort to ensure that plans have enough money to pay benefits when due. There are penalties for failing to meet these requirements. There is no requirement that the employer contribute, except in SIMPLE and safe harbor 401(k)s, money purchase plans, SIMPLE IRAs, and SEPs.

The employer may have to contribute in certain automatic enrollment 401(k) plans. The employer may choose to match a portion of the employee's contributions or to contribute without employee contributions. In some plans, employer contributions may be in the form of employer stock.

Employee Contributions

Generally, employees do not contribute to these plans. Many plans require the employee to contribute in order for an account to be established.

Managing the Investment

Plan officials manage the investment and the employer is responsible for ensuring that the amount it has put in the plan plus investment earnings will be enough to pay the promised benefit. The employee often is responsible for managing the investment of his or her account, choosing from investment options offered by the plan. In some plans, plan officials are responsible for investing all the plan's assets.

Amount of Benefits Paid Upon Retirement

A promised benefit is based on a formula in the plan, often using a combination of the employee's age, years worked for the employer, and/or salary. The benefit depends on contributions made by the employee and/or the employer, performance of the account's investments, and fees charged to the account.

Type of Retirement Benefit Payments

Traditionally, these plans pay the retiree monthly annuity payments that continue for life. Plans may offer other payment options. The retiree may transfer the account balance into an individual retirement account (IRA) from which the retiree withdraws money, or may receive it as a lump sum payment. Some plans also offer monthly payments through an annuity.

Guarantee of Benefits

The Federal government, through the Pension Benefit Guaranty Corporation (PBGC), guarantees some amount of benefits. No Federal guarantee of benefits.

Leaving the Company Before Retirement Age

If an employee leaves after vesting in a benefit but before the plan's retirement age, the benefit generally stays with the plan until the employee files a claim for it at retirement. Some defined benefit plans offer early retirement options. The employee may transfer the account balance to an individual retirement account (IRA) or, in some cases, another employer plan, where it can continue to grow based on investment earnings. The employee also may take the balance out of the plan, but will owe taxes and possibly penalties, thus reducing retirement income. Plans may cash out small accounts."

The U.S. Department of Labor explains the various forms of retirement plans that are available to companies at the following Internet locations:

http://www.dol.gov/ebsa/faqs/faq_compliance_pension.html

http://www.dol.gov/ebsa/publications/wyskapr.html

$&¢

Chapter Twenty-Five

_____R_____

Nonqualified Plans - Types

Nonqualified benefits can be highly useful to any business, and may be employed for many purposes. Nonqualified benefits come in different forms, each with advantages and disadvantages for employers and employees.

Nonqualified plans do not qualify for special tax treatment under IRS laws.

Types of Nonqualified Benefits

Salary Continuation

Under a salary continuation agreement, the employer agrees to continue an executive's salary for a specified period of time. This can create a powerful incentive for key executives to remain with a business.

- This type of plan is often used to supplement the **retirement income** of executives.

- It can also provide benefits in the event of **disability** or **death**.

Because the plan is nonqualified, the sponsoring company has expanded flexibility in plan design. Benefits can be 10% of salary or 200% of salary — for one year, five years, for life, or anything in between.

This type of agreement does *not* normally involve a reduction in current employee pay. It is provided by the employer *in addition* to all other benefits.

Important characteristics of salary continuation include:

- The amount of salary continuation is usually determined by a formula.
  - The agreement can promise a fixed amount, such as: $100,000 per year for fifteen years.
  - The formula to determine benefits can be a percentage of salary or total compensation.
  - Similar to a defined benefit pension, the amount used to determine benefits may be calculated using such measures as an average of the final three or five years' salary, or the average of the three or five years of highest earnings.
- Benefits often have a "years of service" or target date component. For example, benefits may not be earned until an executive has accrued X years of service, or remains employed until X date.
- As with an integrated qualified plan, benefits may be integrated with Social Security.
- Salary continuation may also be integrated with other company benefits.

Salary Reduction (Deferred Compensation)

Deferred compensation typically involves having an executive defer a portion of current pay until some future date. This may be especially attractive if an executive expects to be in a lower tax bracket during retirement.

The employer can make additions to this deferral, in the form of a match or bonus. Matching contributions can help offset the financial risk an employee takes in the event of employer default.

The Mechanics of Salary Reduction

Nonqualified salary reduction plans have many of the same features as qualified salary deferral plans. They also have features not seen in traditional qualified plans. Nonqualified plans usually have:

- A third party administrator who calculates benefits.
- Individual "accounts" with certain investment elements for participants.
  - These can be actual accounts, with segregated assets.
  - They can be shadow accounts, created with mere bookkeeping entries.
  - Earnings can be real and accumulated.
- Earnings can be allocated to employee accounts based upon *hypothetical* performance of an assumed investment, such as an Investment Index.
- Earnings can be a guaranteed amount that is promised by the employer, such as 6% each year.

SERP & Excess Benefit Plans

The two most common types of salary continuation programs are:

- A Supplemental Executive Retirement Plan (SERP).
- An Excess Benefit Plan.

SERP

SERPs typically provide executives a percentage of pay, as with a defined benefit plan. Benefits are normally paid in the event of:

- Retirement,
- Death, or
- Disability.

EXCESS BENEFIT PLAN

An Excess Benefit Plan (also known as a Top-Hat Plan) integrates with an executive's other benefits. This type of plan is normally used for highly compensated executives. In theory, an excess plan compensates for any benefits lost due to the limitations imposed on retirement plans by the Internal Revenue Code.

Excess benefit plans attempt to make up for contributions that would have been made for executives, were the qualified plan limitations not in place.

All *unfunded* excess benefit (Top-Hat) plans, that are established for a "select group of management or highly compensated employees," are subject to minimal ERISA reporting requirements.

Unfunded Top-Hat plans must file a one-time statement about the arrangement with the Department of Labor. They must also be able to provide documentation upon request.

Virtually all nonqualified plans are limited to management and/ or highly compensated employees and are *informally* funded. This is because formal funding creates negative income tax consequences for both the company and the executive.

THE PAYMENT OF BENEFITS

With nonqualified plans, benefits become payable when certain milestones are achieved by the executive. An executive's account will have a calculated value at any given future date. How this value is paid will be determined by the agreement. Payments can take several forms. The most common methods of payment are:

- A lump sum
    - o This may be an agreed-upon figure.
    - o It may be an accumulated amount, based upon actual or theoretical investment returns.
    - o The present value of future benefits, much like a lump-sum payment with a pension, or your state's lottery.
- An annuity
    - o This may be paid in installments over time.
    - o A lump sum may be used to purchase an actual annuity with an insurance company which assumes the payment liability.

Constructive Receipt

Income can be taxable, even if it is not actually received by an executive. If income is "constructively received," it is considered paid. This is a problem that employers need to avoid.

Internal Revenue Code Section 1.451-2(a) outlines the constructive receipt doctrine. This doctrine states that income, even if not actually in a taxpayer's (employee's) possession, is "constructively received" if the taxpayer may draw upon it in any way. In other words, there must be a substantial *risk of forfeiture* for benefits earned under a plan to *avoid* current taxation.

Under the IRS definition, assets are deemed received if "credited to the employees account, set aside, or otherwise made available." Taxation can result, even if an employee has received no distribution of cash, stock or property.

For example: If a company establishes an *irrevocable* trust to hold assets allocated to fund an agreement, this will be deemed constructive receipt, as the risk of forfeiture has been removed. A revocable trust, with some restrictions, may be okay.

Income is not constructively received if an employee's control is subject to *substantial limitations or restrictions*, such as a passage of time before benefits can be enjoyed. For example, if an amount is not payable for five years, termination, or retirement, the benefit will not be currently taxed.

Risk of Forfeiture

Lack of control and imposed *restrictions*, along with company assets being *accessible to corporate creditors*, all help to create the risk of forfeiture needed to make any nonqualified plan work smoothly.

Another useful forfeiture provision is to require that an employee be available for consulting, after the separation of services, in order to receive the promised benefits.

Well drafted plans avoid the constructive receipt of benefits, while still maintaining certain protections for the executive.

Distributions

Plan distributions must be designed to avoid constructive receipt. For example, if an employee is allowed to accelerate payments, or borrow from accounts, this will be considered receipt.

Termination of Employment

Executives typically receive nonqualified benefits in the event of:

- Death,
- Disability, or
- Retirement.

Vesting

Most companies use a vesting schedule. Vesting schedules are used for several purposes:

- The company imposes a vesting schedule to ensure that an employee fulfills the obligations under the agreement. Typically, benefits accrue more significantly as an executive approaches retirement.
- A vesting schedule can help avoid the constructive receipt of benefits.
  - o This allows benefits to accrue without current

taxation to the employee.

Caution:

When an executive becomes vested in benefits, and can demand these benefits, the benefits become *taxable*. Companies must always maintain a risk of forfeiture while an executive works for the company. Otherwise, the purpose of the agreement will be violated.

Employee Protection

You can build employee protection into an agreement in different ways. Most of the protections focus on vesting benefits which happen upon specified events, such as:

- Retirement,
- Death, or
- Disability.

Employer Protection

If you commit valuable resources to a nonqualified plan, you want to make sure that an executive doesn't walk away with your money — until the executive has fulfilled his part of the agreement. Your agreement should include termination provisions in the event that the executive defaults on his part of the bargain.

Funding

Deferred compensation and SERP plans can be fully funded, partially funded, or not funded at all. Regardless of funding, the sponsoring company remains liable to fulfill the obligations of the agreement.

Informally Funded

If benefits are funded, and linked to the agreement, they become taxable whenever an employee becomes "substantially vested" under Code Section 83. Because of this, most non-qualified funding, especially within private businesses, is done on an informal, non-linked basis.

Informal means that the agreement does not mention a specific funding vehicle. The executive may not have direct control over any funding vehicle. Nor, can the executive demand access to funding vehicles under normal circumstances.

Formal Funding

Formally funded plans usually become subject to ERISA vesting and fiduciary requirements. Formal funding creates significant complications, making it unattractive for most companies.

Financing

When productive employees are making long-term financial decisions, they want some measure of security and assurance that their employer's promises will be met.

Sinking Fund

While most plans are not formally funded, they *are* usually financed with some sort of sinking fund. There are a number of ways to set aside assets to fulfill a company's obligation, each with advantages and disadvantages. In all cases, these funds must be accessible to the employer (with some limitations) and available to corporate creditors.

Reserve Accounts With Employee Direction

Larger companies use deferred compensation plans that look and feel much like a 401(k). An employee elects to defer a portion of their current income. This money gets invested. The investment choices in these accounts must be less specific than a 401(k). Employee choices are usually limited to generic accounts, such as equity, bonds, fixed account or money market within a sponsoring mutual fund or insurance company plan.

An ability to choose specific investments may lead to constructive receipt by employees, and immediate taxation.

Corporate Owned Life Insurance

Most nonqualified plans in private companies are "informally" funded with corporate owned life insurance. This holds true for both large and small companies.

Life insurance has a unique set of tax characteristics that give it advantages over other funding vehicles. Life insurance can be used to:

- Provide salary continuation in the event of an executive's death.
- Fund payments in the event of an executive's disability.
- Accumulate assets in a predictable and tax-favored manner.
- Fund an executive's retirement income.
- Provide cost recovery to an employer for benefits paid to executives.
- Satisfy executive fears over security, through life insurance ownership in a "Rabbi Trust."

Rabbi Trust

The first Rabbi Trust was created for a nonqualified plan to benefit a synagogue's rabbi. The trust was established to hold property that was used to finance a deferred compensation plan. Under terms of the trust, the synagogue could not use the trust assets for its general purposes. The trust assets remained available to creditors in the event of financial insolvency.

Since that time, tens of thousands of similar trusts have been utilized by companies for the purpose of protecting assets for employees, without triggering constructive receipt of the property.

When drafted correctly, a Rabbi Trust meets with IRS approval, maintaining non-funding status, while protecting the executive against the unauthorized use of trust assets.

Taxation of Benefits & Compensation

Employee Taxation

Employees that benefit from nonqualified deferred compensation must pay ordinary income tax on benefits in the year that the benefit is actually or constructively received.

Amounts that are deferred from pay are not subject to Medicare or Social Security tax. When received, they are treated as compensation and will be subject to Medicare, Social Security and income taxes at that time. This includes constructive receipt as well as the actual receipt of assets.

Employer Taxation

Employers generally receive a tax deduction in the tax year that benefits are actually or constructively received by an employee. Payments are deductible as long as they meet the "reasonable" standards that are outlined by law.

Chapter Twenty-Six

R

Nonqualified Plans - Summary

Nonqualified Plans

Nonqualified plans, often referred to as deferred compensation (deferred comp), is used by both public and private companies, particularly with senior management. Nonqualified plans are a cost effective, selective benefit that can reward (and retain) key employees.

Because they are not "qualified," this type of benefit has advantages, and disadvantages, when compared to plans that are qualified under ERISA.

Nonqualified plans are used for the following:

- For owners and senior executives in lieu of a qualified plan.

- To provide additional benefits beyond those provided by a company's qualified plans. There are many different types of benefits that can be provided.

- To give the benefits of company ownership without transferring actual ownership of a privately held company.

- To provide customized, tax-deferred benefits which are individually tailored to each person receiving them.

- When a company needs to provide additional incentives to:
  - Recruit talented executives.
  - Reward executives for outstanding service.
  - Retain key personnel.
  - Provide additional retirement benefits over and above company qualified plans.

Advantages

While, nonqualified (deferred compensation) plans do not enjoy favorable tax treatment, they do have other significant advantages over qualified plans. Nonqualified (deferred compensation) plans can be provided for *anyone*, and can provide the following:

- Nonqualified plans allow employers to select who receives benefits, without fear of discrimination.

- Benefits can be unlimited.

- Different benefits can be provided to each executive/ employee.

- IRS and ERISA regulations are minimal.

- Fiduciary reporting and disclosure requirements are minimal.

- Executives are not taxed on monies set aside to fund benefits.

- They can be used to create "golden handcuffs," to keep key personnel from becoming competitors.

- They can be used to create a "golden parachute" with

retirement benefits for executives and/or owners.

- Benefits may become payable when executives enjoy a lower tax bracket than at present.

- Executives may benefit from the compounding of tax deferrals.

- Performance incentives can be built into agreements.

    o Benefits can be tied to such things as profits and sales growth. They can also be linked to department or personal goals, or even the value of an employer's stock.

- Nonqualified benefits can have any vesting schedule. Care must be taken to avoid constructive receipt. This could cause unfavorable tax treatment, long before benefits are paid.

- Partial protection can be created for executives by the use of Rabbi Trusts.

- Assets that are set aside for executives remain on the company balance sheet as a corporate asset.

- There is no legal requirement that forces current assets to be set aside to fund nonqualified agreements. This may help with company cash flow.

Disadvantages

Nonqualified plans discriminate in favor of certain employees. As a result, a sponsoring company will not receive the same *current* favorable tax treatment as it would with a qualified plan — whether the company is making contributions, or simply promising benefits to employees.

While a company cannot take current deductions as they set aside assets for executives, the company may deduct the cost of benefits as they are *paid* to the executive.

This is not an issue for non-profit companies, as they already pay no income taxes.

Note: Companies that use accrual accounting must expense the "present value of future benefits," as they accrue to executives under a nonqualified plan. This is a discussion beyond the scope of this book. Discuss this with your tax and benefit advisors.

Other disadvantages might include:

- To avoid current employee taxation, non-qualified plans must *restrict* the benefits given to selected individuals.

- Benefits that are accrued under a nonqualified plan can only be secured by a company's promise to pay. Assets cannot be segregated for this purpose and shielded from the claims of creditors.

   o If a sponsoring company goes into receivership, assets that have been set aside for executive benefits can be taken to satisfy the claims of senior creditors. If a company goes out of business, executives can lose any and all benefits they have accrued.

   o A Rabbi trust provides a measure of protection to the executive. It prevents the sponsoring company from using such assets for general business purposes.

- Most companies that enter into nonqualified arrangements with executives must still report to the IRS. The reporting can be minimal, however.

- S Corporations, LLCs, LLPs and Partnerships are less

suited to nonqualified plans than traditional C corporations. This is because they are generally taxed at the individual, not the corporate level.

- Employee termination, whether voluntary or forced, may cause the forfeiture of benefits.

  o Executives may demand protection within their agreements against termination for unjust reasons.

- The present value of future benefits must normally be treated as a liability on the corporate balance sheet.

Nonqualified plans provide many benefits — for executives, and the companies that employ them. Care must be taken to structure and fund these agreements properly. When done so, employees have incentive to be productive, while companies have a cost-effective way to keep and reward their most valued workers.

The next chapter discusses the regulation of these plans in greater detail.

$&¢

Chapter Twenty-Seven

R

Deferred Compensation & Section 409A

DEFERRED COMPENSATION & SECTION 409A

Nonqualified plans are an important part of the employee benefit toolbox. They can be essential in attracting and retaining key employees.

Large companies use these agreements regularly. Examine the 8-K disclosure report of any public company and you will find a section devoted to these benefits.

Private companies don't have the same resources as large, public companies. They can't afford such generous mixes of insurance and qualified retirement benefits. However, they must still compete for the same executives.

Private companies can use nonqualified benefits to provide selective compensation to attract and retain employees that are essential to its success. Nonqualified benefits can allow smaller companies to compete effectively with their much larger competition.

The use of nonqualified plans has grown dramatically in recent years. Regulating these plans has grown challenging. Because of this, Congress crafted legislation which must be followed by all companies that offer non-qualified plans.

As part of the American Jobs Creation Act of 2004, Section 409A was added to the Internal Revenue Code.

Section 409A made significant changes to the rules regulating nonqualified deferred compensation. Some of these changes were designed to protect employees against potential abuse by employers. Others were designed to tighten the rules regarding the taxation of benefits, particularly with regard to constructive receipt.

Section 409A expanded the definition of deferred compensation to include *any* agreement that allows an employee to defer compensation from a current tax year to one in the future. Special rules were created for publicly traded companies (which this book won't address). Examples of plans included under this regulation include:

- Elective deferral (traditional deferred compensation) plans.
- Split dollar life insurance plans.
- Severance plans.
- Nonqualified defined benefit plans.
- Expense reimbursement plans.
- Certain stock option and stock rights plans.

409A Changes

Section 409A created new regulations regarding:

- The timing of distributions.
- The timing of deferrals.
- The acceleration of benefits.

Distributions

Under this law, distributions from a nonqualified deferred compensation plan can be made only under certain circumstances. Payments can be made:

- Based upon a fixed schedule or time outlined in the agreement.
- If an employee separates from service.
- If an employee becomes disabled.
- If an employee dies.
- If there is a change in company ownership or a change in effective control.
- If there is an unforeseen emergency.

Deferrals

Section 409A made changes to the *structure* and *timing* of employee deferrals under any deferred compensation arrangement.

Timing — Initial Deferrals

Under Section 409A, employees must now elect to defer compensation in the year *before* the services (under the agreement) are to be performed. The deferral period must be at least five years if deferred payments will be made upon:

- Separation from service.
- Change in company control.
- A specific payment schedule or payment date.

Penalties

If the requirements of Section 409A are breached, employees may be subject to an acceleration of income taxes, plus an *additional* penalty tax of 20%.

Conclusion

The regulations regarding nonqualified deferred compensation are complicated, and must be followed precisely to avoid adverse taxation. When you enter into such agreements, make sure that you are using competent counsel.

If you want to learn more about Section 409A, the following resources will be helpful.

http://www.irs.gov/newsroom/article/0,,id=172883,00.html

http://www.principal.com/nqdc/referenceguide.pdf

Chapter Twenty-Eight

R
_____

Split Dollar Life Insurance

Split Dollar Life Insurance

Split dollar life insurance is a flexible technique that companies use to provide nonqualified benefits to key employees.

Split dollar strategies offer most of the benefits of traditional nonqualified plans, with far more simplicity. Split dollar is also regulated under Section 409A, so care must still be taken to implement it properly.

Life insurance is popular because it provides predictable, low risk cash accumulation. It also provides benefits in the event of disability, plus a lump sum payment in the event of death.

Split Ownership

With split dollar insurance, the payment, ownership and the benefits of a life insurance policy become split between the sponsoring company and the employee. The splitting can occur in different ways, depending upon the individual goals of the employer and the executive.

The splitting of benefits can allow a sponsoring company to provide most of a plan's funding without triggering a taxable event to the employee. Splitting can allow a company to recover its expenditures into a plan. It can also provide tangible current benefits to an employee (such as a current death benefit) at a very low cost.

Advantages of Split Dollar For the Employer:

- It can provide benefits to selected employees.
- Benefits can be tailored to the individual needs of the company and executives.
- There is substantial flexibility in plan design.
- It can provide golden handcuffs or a golden parachute.
- It can provide predictable cash for promised benefits.
- Life insurance has tax advantages over most other investment vehicles.
- Cash values can be used as an emergency reserve for the company.
- No formal IRS approval is needed.
- Minimal IRS and tax reporting is required.
- Recordkeeping costs are minimal.

Advantages For the Employee:

- Split dollar plans can be used to supplement retirement income.
- Employees can accumulate cash in a tax favored manner.
- Plans can be designed to help the employee in the event of disability.
- Substantial tax free benefits can be available to the employee's family at death.
- Plans can protect against future un-insurability.
- Executives can leverage personal outlays into a life in-

surance policy.

How It Works

Split dollar arrangements involve the purchase of a life insurance policy, with the executive being the insured. The payments (premiums) and benefits of the policy then become shared by the employer and the executive.

There are two primary types of split dollar arrangements.

Endorsement Split Dollar:

- With endorsement split dollar, the employer owns the policy and pays the premiums.

- The employer retains an interest in the policy equal to the greater of cash values or the premiums paid.

- Through an endorsement in the policy, the remaining death benefit can be assigned to the employee's heirs.

- The executive may pay the annual imputed economic benefit (the PS-58 or the annual term rates). The death benefit may be assigned to a spouse, or a specific entity, such as an irrevocable trust or family partnership. This keeps the life insurance benefits tax free to heirs. Alternatively, the executive (or entity) can pay the tax on the imputed annual benefit.

- When the executive retires, the policy may be used to pay supplementary income under a nonqualified arrangement.

Collateral Assignment:

- With collateral assignment, the corporation enters into an agreement with the executive to assist with the payments of life insurance premiums.

- The executive purchases a life insurance policy on the executive's life.

- The executive retains all ownership rights.

- The employer pays most or all of the premiums.

- The executive "collaterally assigns" a portion of the death benefit and cash values to the employer. This amount is generally equal to all or a portion of the employer's premiums.

- As in endorsement split dollar, the employee will pay (at least) the annual imputed economic benefit of the life insurance to maintain the tax free status in the event of death.

- At death, the executive's heirs receive a tax-free lump sum distribution of their portion of the death benefit.

- At retirement, the executive terminates the collateral agreement with the employer.
  - The employer may forgive any or all monies owed for its premium payments.
    - ❖ This will be a taxable event. The employee may withdraw or borrow against policy values to pay any taxes due.
  - The employee can take loans or withdrawals from the policy to repay the employer for premiums it has made toward the policy.

Split Dollar and Estate Planning

Split dollar planning can also become a sophisticated estate planning tool with owners, family members or highly paid executives. For example, with endorsement split dollar, the death benefit portion of a life insurance policy can be assigned to a spouse, an irrevocable life insurance trust, or a family limited partnership. These entities must pay the annual "term" portion of the policy. In the event of death before retirement, the life insurance proceeds will pass tax free to the spouse, a trust, or partnership set up for heirs.

The following chart shows a few examples of how split dollar life insurance may be utilized for maximum benefit. Talk to a qualified financial professional to explore the many uses of split dollar life insurance.

Split Dollar Alternatives

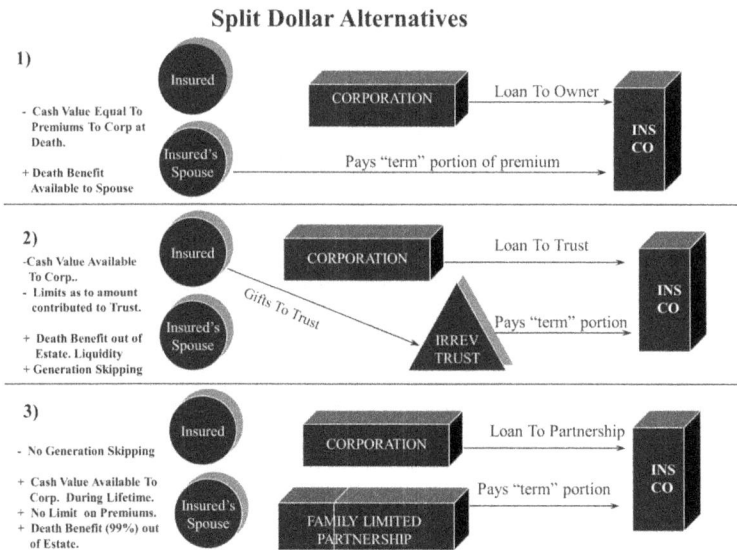

Summary

Split dollar plans can be a valuable, cost-effective tool when seeking ways to attract and retain key executives in a cost effective, simplified manner. It can also be a valuable tool for sophisticated estate and financial planning.

The IRS provides tax information at the following Internet addresses:

https://www.irs.gov/irb/2003-46_IRB/ar08.html

https://www.irs.gov/Businesses/Corporations/Split-Dollar-Life-Insurance-Audit-Technique-Guide-(03-2005)

Chapter Twenty-Nine

R

Qualified & Nonqualified Plan Summary

RETIREMENT BENEFITS SUMMARY:

WHICH RETIREMENT PLAN IS RIGHT FOR YOUR BUSINESS?

We have discussed many types of benefit and retirement plans. Your executive team will decide which plan, or which combination of plans, is most appropriate for your company. In order to help with your decision, the different plans are outlined below, along with the circumstances that might lead to their use by a company.

Defined Benefit Pension — Best For:

- Companies with stable earnings and solid financials, particularly those who have already implemented other plans, like a 401(k).

- Smaller companies with older executives who want to set aside large sums in a tax favored manner.

- Professional corporations, and the self-employed, who want to shelter greater income and protect assets.

Money Purchase Pension — Best For:

- Companies with stable earnings and solid financials.
- Companies with bargaining units.
- Companies that want to provide greater retirement benefits beyond profit sharing and 401(k) plans.

Profit Sharing — Best For:

- Companies that want to supplement existing pension plans.
- Companies that want to create profit incentives for employees.
- Companies that have less predictable profits.
- Companies that want to set aside greater funds for key executives.

ESOP — Best For:

- Business owners that want to sell company stock in a tax-favored manner.
- Owners that want to create tax-deductible payments for company financing.
- Owners that want to give stock to employees without giving up control of the company.

Integrated Pension & Profit Sharing — Best For:

- Companies that want to allocate a greater percentage of corporate contributions toward more highly compensated employees.

Age Weighted Profit Sharing & New Comparability — Best For:

- Companies that want to allocate more company contributions toward older and more highly compensated executives.

- Privately held companies that want to set aside qualified funds for the ownership and management groups.

401(k)

- With today's technology and pricing, **every** company, regardless of size, should consider offering a 401(k) plan to employees. 401(k) plans are an essential benefit for any company that must compete for productive employees.

- A 401(k) can include company matching and profit sharing contributions.

Safe Harbor 401(k) — Best For:

- Companies that want to make employer contributions.

- Companies with executives that want to maximize deferrals into the plan.

- Companies that want to reduce administrative costs and requirements.

Nonqualified Plans — Best For:

- Companies that want to attract and retain key executives on a selective basis.

- Companies that want to reward specific employees.

- Companies that want to allocate excess corporate resources toward a select group of executives.

Split Dollar Life Insurance — Best For:

- Companies that want to attract and retain key executives on a selective basis.

- Companies that want reward specific employees.

- Companies that want to allocate excess corporate resources toward a select group of executives.

- Companies that want to minimize regulation.

- Companies that want to simplify recordkeeping & expenses.

- Companies that want predictable cash accumulation.

- Owner/Executives that want to employ sophisticated estate and financial planning by using company assets.

Chapter Thirty

_____R_____

Building A 401(k)

BUILDING A 401(k) PLAN

Navigating the myriad government regulations surrounding retirement plans is stressful and distracting. While keeping compliant, companies can fall into the trap of robotic adherence to regulations.

Freedom and creativity can become overwhelmed by logic and structure. As regulations dominate employer thinking, it is easy to lose sight of the most important part of any plan—the employees.

In this section of the book, we explore how *human nature* drives saving and investment behavior. We will review how unconscious, inner instincts stop many Americans from saving enough for retirement.

This book will discuss human nature, as it relates to saving for the future. It will then illustrate how to adapt a 401(k) plan to natural, human instincts. This will help you optimize your plan for maximum employee benefit and satisfaction.

Let's review the reasons why you offer a plan in the first place.

The Fundamental Reasons For A 401(k) Plan

The primary reasons that employers offer a 401(k) plan are as follows:

- To Attract & Retain Quality Employees.
  - Retirement plans were first offered by the large companies. They were used as a recruiting and retention tool. Smaller companies must compete with large companies for the best workers.
- More Profits—Less Headaches.
  - High quality workers seek companies that offer a 401(k). These employees work harder and longer, and take less time off from the job. They create fewer problems in the workplace, especially if a company can afford to let their less productive employees seek employment more suited to their abilities and drive.
- For Employee Benefit.
  - Why are employees attracted to retirement plans? Because they *need* them. Natural, human behavior causes many people to procrastinate with their saving, sometimes all the way to retirement age. Retirement plans, especially if employers are paying into the plan, fill an important investment void for employees. This leads to greater personal contentment and greater productivity.

NEXT SECTION

With the preceding goals in mind, the following pages of this book will:

- Show you how to Design and Manage a 401(k) for Optimal Employee Outcome.

- Provide a simple Step-by-Step Guide on how employers may Double Employee Participation and Wealth Accumulation in their 401(k) plans.

- Explain Fiduciary Obligations—And How To Reduce Fiduciary Liability.

  ○ Recommend What Duties To Sub Out To Professionals.

$&¢

Chapter Thirty-One

R

Human Nature & 401(k) Participation

HUMAN NATURE: IT AFFECTS PARTICIPATION

Employees know that they *should* be saving more for retirement. Intellectually, they *want* to save and invest. Emotionally they *can't*, so they *don't*.

Employers must help employees overcome their natural, instinctual failures. For most employers, this means altering the operational *and* emotional architecture of their 401(k) plans.

KEY CHALLENGES

There are many challenges facing employees as they attempt to save for retirement. Just as there are challenges, there are effective strategies to overcome them.

FEAR

One of the main reasons that employees don't save for retirement is because of fear. Fear is an instinctual emotion with enormous power. 401(k) plans must help overcome natural employee fears.

THE UNKNOWN

Humans are hard-wired to fear the unknown. It is one of our basic instincts for survival.

Survival instincts protected early man from outside dangers. Now, these same instincts can stop employees from participating in a retirement plan.

If employees don't *fully understand a plan*, it will remain an unknown. This can elicit instinctual fear, and prevent employees from investing. Everything about a 401(k) should be fully understood by employees — especially the provisions put in place to help protect and accumulate their money.

MARKET FEARS

Nobody can predict movements of the stock market. Investors fear losing money. Accounts that are invested for gain *will* lose money, on occasion. Sometimes, they will lose a lot. Without the proper perspective, many employees will find other, less beneficial uses for their money.

Some people battle a strong, almost uncontrollable aversion to risk. Emotional responses can cause these individuals to fight the *intellectual* desire to put money into a retirement plan. Such employees must overcome their emotional fear before they can save for retirement. Employers can help them do so.

DISTRACTIONS

When faced with a challenging task, many of us find busywork to distract us from what we must do. We make excuses. We procrastinate. Retirement planning is one of the most difficult challenges we face. It is easy to divert attention from it, to the point where it never gets done. 401(k) design must reduce, or

eliminate, distractions that deter or prevent employee participation.

TRUST IN THE PLAN

People fear losing (control of) their money to others. While
employees might trust their employer, they might still fear losing their money to theft, by a person or company involved
with the plan. Employers must explain the safeguards that
are in place to protect employee funds. Employers can utilize
many effective mechanisms to reduce and eliminate the real
and debilitating preventers of employee wealth creation.

MAKE IT REAL

While part of a plan's education process must be designed to
overcome employee fears, other parts must *induce* fear.

Your plan must educate employees in a way that **reduces** the
fear of investing. You must **replace** this fear with the fear of
not investing enough.

URGENCY

When retirement is 20 or 30 years away, it is hard for some
employees to feel the urgency to save. A lack of urgency
makes it difficult for employees to overcome their instinctual
roadblocks.

When you make the need for saving "real," by triggering an
emotional reaction, you will achieve higher participation and
more satisfied participants.

MAKE IT VISCERAL

If you have had business or sales training, you understand
the need to arouse emotions when you need to get something

done. Sports coaches deliver inspiring speeches to motivate their players. Technology executives prepare elaborate product launches that stimulate imagination and emotions.

Envision Steve Jobs standing on stage and speaking to tens of thousands of excited acolytes. Emotional power and branding helped drive Apple to become the biggest company on the planet. Successful retail companies, like Wal-Mart and Disney, have regular morning rallies to create positive employee feelings. Advertising executives study how to associate products with visceral, human reactions. We are driven by our emotions.

Effective 401(k)s are built use employee emotions as an ally, not an adversary.

MAKE IT EASY

If you make it easy to participate in a 401(k), you will have higher participation. This is simple logic, backed up by facts.

Companies make it too challenging for employees to enroll in their 401(k)s. They make it too difficult for employees to increase their contributions.

Many employers just don't understand the subtle emotional nuances that can drive dramatically human behavior. At least yet.

The next section presents enrollment strategies that can dramatically enhance employee participation in any 401(k) plan.

PLAN ENROLLMENT

Your plan enrollment procedures may be simple *tactically*; they may not be easy *emotionally*. Filling out forms is easy. Filling out forms for a retirement plan is not. A plan's enrollment paperwork and computer applications might be simple.

But, for many employees, even basic paperwork is too much. Some employees simply can't *overcome their core human nature* to do the minimal paperwork necessary to achieve optimum utilization.

Employers can make better accommodations for employees—both physically and emotionally. When companies make 401(k) deferrals easier, higher plan participation and higher deferral rates become *inevitable.* Participation soars.

MAKE DEMANDS OF EMPLOYEES *AND* OF MANAGEMENT

When a company sets high goals, and breaks those goals into manageable steps, great things happen—for employers, employees, and their retirement plans.

BE A GOOD MODEL

The days of the benevolent employer are not gone. But they have changed. Companies cannot afford generous pensions and large profit sharing contributions. But they can still do things to help employees, usually without great expense.

Employers want the best for their employees. So, if employees are not able to save effectively on their own, a thoughtful employer takes steps to help them achieve greater financial freedom.

When a 401(k) sponsor makes things easy, explains information clearly, sets reasonable expectations, rewards positive behaviors and discourages negative behaviors, extraordinary changes occur.

FIGHT MYOPIA

Humans are built to focus on the moment—today, rather than tomorrow. For some, retirement planning doesn't become today, until it is too late.

When we begin our working careers, we give attention to our coffee, the latest new phone, stylish clothing and a nice car. Retirement is too many years away.

In middle age, we might focus our energies on a house, entertainment, or our children. We can be too busy to plan.

Finally, once life slows down and the kids move away (if they ever do), it becomes time to think about retirement. By then, it's too late.

EMPLOYEE VISUALIZATION

If one cannot visualize the result of making current sacrifices, it is harder to make those sacrifices. Why sacrifice today for an amorphous "someday," when the lure of a tasty latte, snack or another new car takes emotional precedence?

When we think of ourselves in the future, our brains are naturally wired to see this as *someone else*, a stranger. This book will present research that will show you how to use new, novel methods to help your employees better see themselves more easily in retirement.

REALITY

When retirement becomes as real as work, kids and coffee, it becomes a priority. When employees begin planning for themselves, not some stranger in their minds, sacrifice seems more worthwhile.

APPROPRIATE EDUCATION

When employees fully understand the enrollment, accumulation, and the distribution phases of retirement saving, they dramatically increase their plan participation.

FIGHT INERTIA

It is easier for people to do what they have always done (save too little) than it is to enact change. People dislike change. They are afraid to change. People procrastinate. This leads to inaction.

An effective 401(k) sponsor learns how to overcome inertia, and get things rolling in the right direction.

A LOOK INSIDE

If we take a closer look *inside* the human body, we might learn more effective ways to manage behavior on the *outside.*

Let's begin.

$&¢

Chapter Thirty-Two

R

Human Nature — A Brief Overview

HUMAN NATURE & INVESTING: OUR HARD-WIRING

Why is it that the majority Americans are dependent upon *work* and the *government* for their "retirement" income? Why do so many people ignore professional advice? Why do most Americans put off saving enough until it is far too late?

There are many reasons that adequate saving and investing doesn't happen for most individuals. But when the onion gets peeled to its very core, the answer is simple—human nature.

Our bodies are hard-wired to make decisions emotionally, not logically. We back up emotional decisions with logic, but the decisions themselves are generally driven by feelings.

We do things that make us feel good. We don't like doing things that make us feel uncomfortable.

Have you ever found yourself making a "gut reaction" against all logic? Today's neuroscience research shows how simple probiotics in the gut can influence behavior. So do many other things that we cannot see. A short explanation of how the internal biome influences behavior can be found here: http://www. apa.org/monitor/2012/09/gut-feeling.aspx

HUMAN PHYSIOLOGY

Physiology is where investing starts. When analyzed closely, we will find that many of our bodies' important decisions are made *for* us, not *by* us with conscious brain activity.

Our central nervous systems send continual signals to the rest of our bodies. Hormones and neurotransmitters are released. Feedback is received and adjustments are made. Every second of every day, we send and receive messages that raise and lower our blood pressure and heart rate. Silent signals control our pupil dilation and our vasoconstriction. We feel relaxed; we feel stressed; we feel anger and pain — often without conscious thought.

These subconscious reactions evolved over thousands of years. They helped us survive. They don't always help us save and invest. Sometimes, they stop us completely.

STRESS

If we are going to make dramatic changes in investment behavior, we must create changes on the *physiological* level.

When the stress of *not* saving becomes greater than the stress of *taking short-term risk*...When the stress caused by *not saving* overpowers today's emotional desire for pleasure, taking positive action *reduces* stress.

Such a physical change in behavior can take place with the right type of *education*.

ACTION

Nothing happens without positive action. Saving can't happen without the conscious *decision* to save. Investment growth can't happen without the decision to undertake *risk*.

Once present and future needs have been *quantified*...Once the methodology and the risks are fully *understood*...People can develop a saving and investment *plan* that meets their individual financial goals, *without* causing undue stress.

GOALS

We are more productive when we have specific, tangible, reachable goals. When large goals are set, they can seem difficult to achieve. They can appear impossible. When big goals are broken down into achievable, stair-step actions, they become manageable. Short-term sacrifice becomes more palatable when it is part of a greater plan.

THE NUMBER

THE NUMBER is a long-term financial target to be reached years in the future.

When an employee first calculates the amount needed to retire as desired, it is a monster—a huge, imposing sum that seems too intimidating to even attempt to approach.

When an employee calculates that their number is $2,000,000, but that employee has just $10,000 in savings, it may seem an impossible task. It can appear hopeless, and not worth the sacrifice. Some employees will want to quit before they begin.

By understanding human nature, plan sponsors can **present important information in a manner better suited to achieving positive results.**

When broken down into manageable, achievable steps, an employee's number can become a positive motivator.

When a $2,000,000 number is converted into 10% of current pay, or $20 a day, it becomes manageable. $2 million frightens employees. Being automatically enrolled in a plan and then signing a paper allocating a 10% deferral into a growth model, is easy. Better financial security becomes almost inevitable.

Chapter Thirty-Three
_____R_____
The Human Condition

THE HUMAN CONDITION

Who's In Charge?

We like to think that we make major, life-altering decisions with our intellect. We rebel against the thought that our decisions come from hidden command centers that are out of our control — that we are driven by emotions we can't see or manage.

We might tell ourselves that success comes from a desire to succeed. And that lack of achievement comes from a lack of effort and discipline. This can true — effort does breed success. But we are also driven by chemical reactions that result from personal genetic differences, combined with our life-long experiences. Each person reacts to the world in their own unique way.

No one fully understands what goes on deep inside our bodies and brains. Most of us are mostly unaware of the many bio-chemical mechanisms that drive important decisions.

Human hard-wiring evolved over thousands of years. But the wiring that served us well in the stone age can become a detriment in modern society.

Knowledge of human motivation can help employers understand what drives employees to take *positive* (rather than negative) action, what will make them participate. The following hyperlink leads to an article published in the Harvard Business Review. This article discusses the managerial implications of evolutionary psychology, and how businesses can better adapt to how employees naturally behave.

https://hbr.org/1998/07/how-hardwired-is-human-behavior

So — our minds are directed by neurotransmitters and hormones. We feel their effects — love, joy, fear and excitement. Especially stress. When it comes to investing for the future, many people can't get their neurotransmitters to work for positive results.

These chemical reactions, the ones we feel but can't see, that drive investment behavior. By controlling these emotions and reactions (no easy task), *any* individual can affect investment behavior, and achieve greater financial security.

FEELINGS: THE KEY TO MOTIVATION

Decisions are made on two levels. We *see* the first level, *conscious thought*. We don't see the second level. This is the *unconscious*. The unconscious is has a mind of its own, and is driven by emotions. These emotions drive our behavior, regardless of what we might *think*.

When our conscious thought does not align with our unconscious emotions, *nothing positive happens*.

If we don't feel right in our "gut," our primeval, non-thinking self, we will hesitate to take action against it. We can know something all we want, but if something doesn't feel right, we will try to avoid it.

Control

We control our own actions. But outside factors *always* get in the way. We must continually *adapt* to events around us. The government makes new laws. Technology and competition alter business practices. Accidents happen in our lives that we can't predict.

Unforeseeable events happen *inside* us every day, too. We just don't see them. If someone cuts us off in traffic, we may feel anger. If someone compliments our work performance, our clothing or our haircut, we might feel a sudden, blushing satisfaction. Feelings come without conscious thought. They come without intention.

Our most important financial decisions are influenced by unconscious thought. Therefore, a perceived lack of effort, as defined by non-participation in a 401(k), may not stem from a lack of willpower or intent. It may come from emotional forces hidden out of sight. Financial decisions may be influenced by a natural predisposition toward stress, personal traumas, or emotional responses triggered by unconscious events.

WE CAN REPROGRAM OUR BEHAVIOR

As we are all unique, we are also much the same. Our brains are driven by electrical signals, much like a computer. Like a computer, we can *program* our brains to override negative behaviors. We can program our "inner workings" (avoidance of saving) to behave more like our "outer workings" (the desire for financial security).

With proper structure and training, employees will redirect their behavior to match what their rational, thinking brains *know* is best.

Greater financial security is possible. It just requires change — from employers.

401(K) CHANGE

Effective 401(k) management addresses what we don't see, as much as what we do see.

RADICAL IMPROVEMENT

When employers learn how to influence *basic human nature,* radical improvements in saving and investment behavior will naturally occur.

Chapter Thirty-Four

_____R_____

Modern Portfolio Theory & Human Nature

MODERN PORTFOLIO THEORY—HUMAN NATURE IN ACTION

When talking about investments, financial advisors will inevitably reference the analytic tools developed through Modern Portfolio Theory (MPT). MPT put Harry Markowitz, its founder, on the Mount Rushmore of investing. It gave him a Nobel Prize.

MPT is used throughout the world to measure investment return and risk. With the help of MPT, model portfolios are constructed by virtually every major financial institution. MPT helps portfolio managers seek the greatest return, given the risk (emotions) that investors are willing to assume. (Note: MPT is examined more closely in the companion education book, *Making Cent$ of Investing*.)

DO AS I SAY, NOT AS I DO

In one of his many interviews, Professor Markowitz made an astonishing admission. When it came to investing his own retirement plan money, he once had difficulty following his own, detailed analysis. Instead of investing with reasoned intellect, Markowitz yielded to his uneducated *emotions*.

Dr. Markowitz admitted to investing his own 403(b) retirement money to "minimize his potential loss," rather than achieve "optimal gain."

Instead of using past history to construct the most efficient investment mix for the future, Markowitz placed half of his money into stocks and half in bonds. This way, he surmised, if stocks or bonds did poorly, the other half would (hopefully) fare better.

Markowitz's models could predict investment results, but they could not *guarantee* it. So, Markowitz allowed his emotions to make his investment choice. Rational thought could not overrule his subconscious. He played it safe and sacrificed his long-term growth potential.

As an accomplished professor with other benefits, Dr. Markowitz could afford to hedge in his 403(b). After starting an actual hedge fund, among other profitable business entities, Markowitz could afford to invest any darned way he wanted.

Unfortunately, most Americans don't have that luxury. To achieve financial security, most employees can't play it safe, and invest for greater long-term gain.

Chapter Thirty-Five

R
Bio Plan Design

EDUCATION & PLAN DESIGN

The most effective 401(k)s reduce employee fear of investing. They also increase employee motivation to save.

This can be done in two ways:

- Through proper education, and

- With plan design.

Education can reprogram fear to create positive *motivation,* rather than stressful *avoidance*.

Plan designs can redirect emotional stressors. Proper design can make inertia into a positive force. Greater financial security will naturally follow.

CHEMISTRY & EMOTIONS

Proper retirement and investment education can, literally, change a body's inner chemistry.

Effective education can make investing *less* stressful than maintaining the status quo. Saving can then become habit-forming. Better financial security elicits a reward response. This makes employees feel happy.

Simply offering a competitive 401(k) plan is not enough.

401(k)s must be offered to employees in low-stress ways that encourage positive employee action.

Chapter Thirty-Six

R

Motivation

MOTIVATION

Motivation is critical to proper saving and investing for retirement. Without motivation, nothing gets done. It's just that
simple.

Motivation comes in two basic forms:

- Positive, and

- Negative.

Investment education should create both.

Education should motivate employees to save. When employees are motivated to save, they invest more money toward retirement.

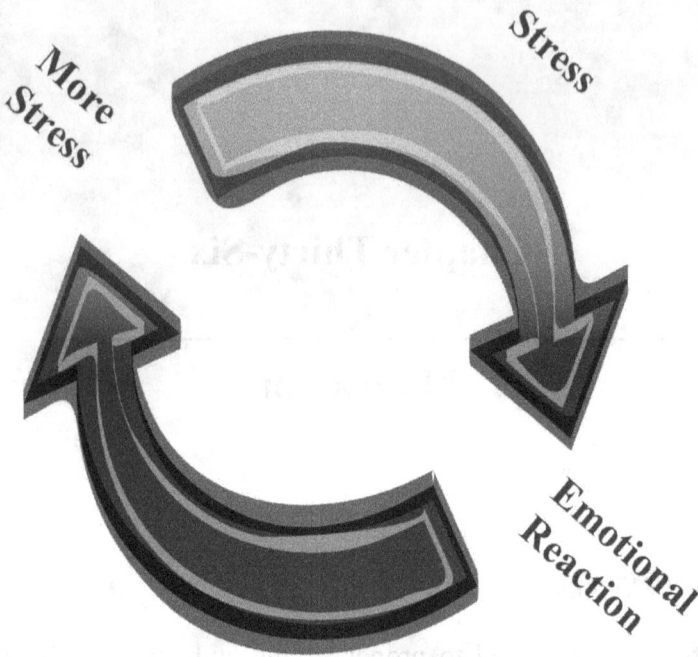

NEGATIVE MOTIVATION — FEAR

For some people, investing can create a circular loop of stressful emotions that never ends. The fear of loss causes stress. This creates inaction. Inaction causes more stress.

For some who do invest, a drop in investment values can cause stress, which causes even more stress. And so on.

We fear making mistakes. We fear losing money. But we can't accumulate the assets we'll need in retirement unless we take that risk.

When we don't understand something, we fear it, and we avoid it. When the gut says "no," we say, "No!"

POSITIVE MOTIVATION

When we look at things intellectually, and our emotions agree, positive action becomes easy. Then it becomes habit.

EMOTIONAL BALANCE

The following pages demonstrate how to create a 401(k) that reprograms employee emotions into a positive form. You will learn how to present information in a manner that helps employees invest with better physical and emotional balance.

When employees understand that short-term loss is a necessary, and natural, part of earning long-term gain, they feel less stress when they lose money in the short-run. When investment loss is seen as an opportunity, rather than a crisis, employees lose the stress of investing today.

When saving and investing for retirement finally makes sense, it will feel right. Employees will then save and invest far more.

When employers understand the role that emotions play in retirement planning, it becomes easier to understand why many participation strategies fail, while others succeed.

NEGATIVE EMOTION — AVOIDANCE

When 401(k) investing causes stress, employees avoid it.

The fear of loss (stress) can be overcome with 401(k) education. If not done correctly, your employees will never approach their saving potential.

ROUTINE CHANGE

The fear of loss is not the only thing that prevents employee participation. For many individuals, *any change in routine*, no matter how small, can cause enough stress to stop action.

Simple acts, like choosing investments and filling out paper-work, can create enough stress to cause employees to avoid participation.

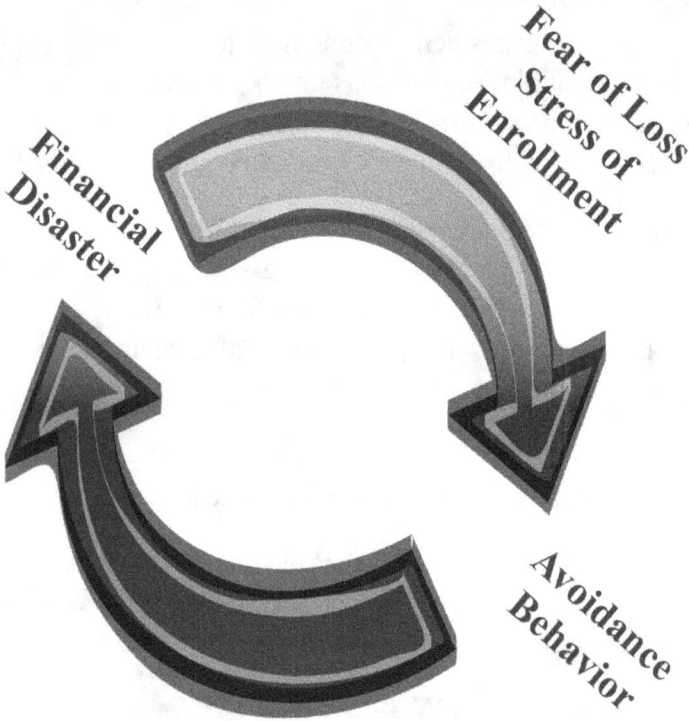

When a plan sponsor reduces the stress of investing, employees will participate more often and with a higher percentage deferral.

AN OPTIMAL 401(K) MAKES IT LESS STRESSFUL *TO* INVEST THAN *NOT TO* INVEST.

Successful plan sponsors change the inner landscape of human motivators and stressors. They create *new* motivators. They eliminate negative, stressful ones.

Successful plan sponsors reduce the stress response of enrolling. They reduce the stress of investing.

Through proper plan design, employers can make it less stressful for employees to participate. Proper education can change the focus of investing. By doing both, companies can create dramatic improvements in participation rates—usually beyond what they ever thought was possible.

$&C

Chapter Thirty-Seven

R

Positive Motivation

POSITIVE MOTIVATION

We have reviewed how investment motivation can be doused by fear and stress. You must find a way to reduce these negative emotions. When you reduce employee fear and stress, positive action results.

Let's take a closer look at what compels positive action.

Savings Motivation.

When we forego spending today, and invest for the future, we do so because we are *motivated*. We are moving *toward* something, not *away* from it. When we want something more in the *future*, than what we want *today*, we will take steps to achieve it.

Maslow's Hierarchy Of Needs

Once our most basic needs are met, we fulfill higher, more complex needs

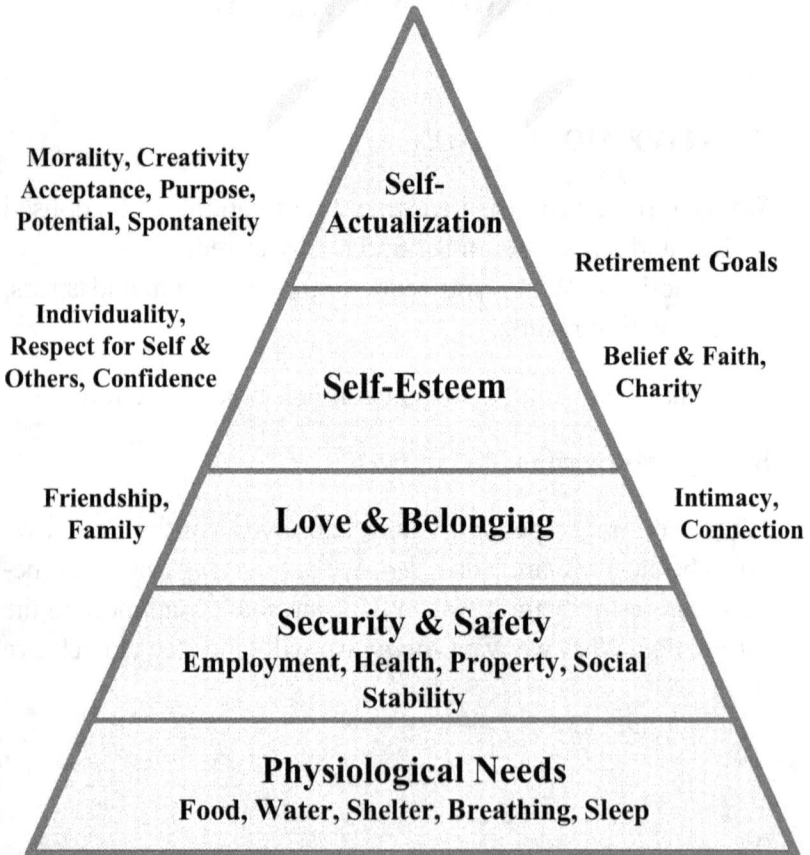

Morality, Creativity Acceptance, Purpose, Potential, Spontaneity

Self-Actualization

Retirement Goals

Individuality, Respect for Self & Others, Confidence

Self-Esteem

Belief & Faith, Charity

Friendship, Family

Love & Belonging

Intimacy, Connection

Security & Safety
Employment, Health, Property, Social Stability

Physiological Needs
Food, Water, Shelter, Breathing, Sleep

MASLOW'S HIERARCHY OF NEEDS

In 1943, a psychologist by the name of Abraham Maslow postulated that humans are motivated to fulfill certain needs. Maslow believed that we manage our needs in an organized fashion. He placed human needs upon a pyramid, with our most basic needs at the bottom, and our most sophisticated needs on top. He theorized that we satisfy our needs from the bottom up.

According to Maslow, our most basic needs are air, food, water, sex, shelter, warmth and sleep. Only when these needs are met, can we begin to address our other, higher needs.

The next level of needs revolve around safety—our need for laws, limits, stability and order, shelter and freedom from fear. This includes our need for *current* and *future* financial security.

The next priority includes our need to be loved and to belong. We seek friendship, romance, family and good working relationships. This comes *after* financial security.

Maslow's fourth order of need is self-esteem, our desire for excellence—mastery of our work and hobbies, achievement (even dominance), status, independence, prestige and self-respect.

According to Maslow, our highest needs can only be attained once the bulk of our other needs are met. If we are cold and starving, we don't care much about self-esteem, or anything else. This is one reason why free meals are provided to many students in school.

HIGH PRIORITY NEEDS

Financial security is one of our most **basic needs**—one we seek to meet before most others.

When we enjoy current creature comforts, it is easy to prepare for future ones, by investing today. This is why participation is highest among the most highly-paid employees. A lesser-paid-employee will feel torn between providing for the basic needs of today versus those of tomorrow.

If one's income is low, it will seem difficult to divert current funds for future benefit. Future financial security must come at the expense of meeting today's other, basic needs.

But our *future* financial security is *just as important* as our current financial security. When employees fully understand the poor state of their future finances, they *will* take action to improve it today. Employees want to meet their most basic needs. Today *and* in the future.

It is possible to radically increase participation among lower-paid employees. When employers change the employee motivators, plan participation can be increased by 100% or more.

DESIGN YOUR 401(K) WITH POSITIVE MOTIVATORS

STAIR-STEP ACHIEVEMENT

Denis Waitley, Ph.D. has written numerous books on motivation and achievement (Psychology of Winning, The Seeds of Greatness, etc.). When training Olympic athletes, Waitley implemented some of the same strategies that companies should use when designing and managing a 401(k).

Waitley and his team knew that when a goal is far away (such as winning a gold medal in four years) it is difficult to remain motivated, and fully committed. But if the long-term goal is broken into many, short-term, achievable goals and workouts, it is easier to remain focused, to stimulate motivation and continue training.

It is the same with investing for retirement. Each time we accomplish a goal, even if it is a small one, we become motivated to achieve the next one.

Stair-step achievement toward savings goals

INVESTING AND MOTIVATION

When employees make small contributions and see them grow, employees will become motivated to increase participation.

When a quarterly statement shows a 5% gain on $10,000, it creates a rewarding experience. When a statement shows savings accumulation, it creates positive motivation to save even more.

Increased financial security reduces stress and stimulates the release of body chemicals that make us feel good.

A well designed 401(k) will help create employee feelings of well-being, all from accumulating money for a comfortable retirement.

PRE-PLANNING THE FUTURE

Waitley also demonstrates how our bodies can feel the effects of achievement, even *before* we achieve it. This is critical to understanding the motivations behind participating in a 401(k).

Just like an Olympic athlete or golfer closes her eyes to visualize a shot, pre-plays a gymnastics routine or a slalom run, employees can pre-play their financial security and comfortable retirement.

When a 401(k) builds structural and educational attributes to enhance positive motivators and reduces negative motivators, employees become more prone to invest. This includes less highly paid employees.

MAKE YOUR 401(K) REWARDING

When a 401(k) plan takes the stress out of enrollment and participation, dramatic increases in wealth accumulation occur.

When employees are continually rewarded, by matching contributions, ongoing education and lifetime statements, a retirement plan will fulfill financial *and* emotional needs.

When education reduces the stress of investing, an employee's focus will change to the positive qualities of saving for retirement.

It may seem odd to think of hidden motivators when designing and implementing a retirement plan. But understanding what causes motivation, and what stops it, will help you improve the saving behavior of your company's employees.

The next chapter will discuss effective plan design, education and communication strategies for your 401(k). You should notice how this book's recommendations embrace human nature as an ally, to help create greater financial security for all. It repeats these recommendations in different ways, so that more people will hear the message.

As we progress, hopefully this will make more sense.

Chapter Thirty-Eight

R

Building The Plan

BUILDING THE PLAN

People move *away* from stress and *toward* reward. This impacts how they save and invest for retirement.

Employees want to save more for retirement, but hormones and neurotransmitters get in the way.

Doesn't it make sense to design a 401(k) that allows human nature to *assist* rather than *thwart* retirement saving? Here is how to do it:

- Make The Decision That You Want To Help Employees Achieve Financial Independence.

    - Make this goal part of your investment policy statement. Then implement the goal.

- Change Your Enrollment Architecture to include Automatic Enrollment.

    - With automatic enrollment, employees must opt *out* of your plan, rather than in. This makes inertia into an ally, not an adversary. Human nature will help employees save more, not less. An enrollment goal of **90%** should be a target.

- Change to a 6% Minimum Default Deferral.

  o For many employees, this will remove the stress of choosing a deferral rate. Employees can still opt out of the plan. They usually won't.

- Implement Future Enrollment For All Opt-Outs.

  o If at first you don't succeed...Many employees won't opt out a second time. Then, as their savings grow, reward chemistry becomes a retirement partner.

- Build Automatic Deferral Increases Into Your Plan.

  o This feature uses inertia to help build employee financial security. While employees can opt out of automatic deferral increases, they usually won't. Set an **average deferral goal of 10%** as a minimum target for your plan.

- Make it Easier to Stay In Your Plan than to opt out. Schedule Opt-out Interviews. Make employees walk to get opt-out paperwork. Don't send it to them in an email, drop it on their desk or let them click a mouse. (Make sure that you check with your plan provider about this first. Plan laws may vary and they certainly change.)

- If you can't use automatic enrollment, then you should implement Easy Enroll Architecture for your plan. Easy enroll allows employees to enroll now, and do the paperwork later.

- Design Your Company Match For Optimum Participation.

- ○ Most matching plans can be reengineered for better employee participation.
- Simplify Your Plan. Simplicity works.
- Change the Choice Architecture on Investments.
  - ○ Studies show that investors fare poorly when investing on their own. Individual equity investors earn about half the return that they would earn with a passive index. This is because emotions often drive investment decisions. Plan design should funnel employees toward asset allocation models, **with a goal of 90%**.
- Use Information Architecture.
  - ○ Create or implement age-based or risk-based asset allocation models that approach the efficient frontier (Modern Portfolio Theory). Run the numbers if you can.
- Present Clear and Understandable Education.
  - ○ Your plan education should be designed to elicit positive investment decisions, and create educated emotions that help employees achieve their most important goals.
  - ○ Education should be designed to elicit emotions from accurate facts, not uninformed bias or fear of the unknown.
  - ○ **Make the fear of not investing greater than the fear of short-term investment loss.**
- Use Visualization Techniques.
- Hold meetings.
- Have employees on your Investment Policy Board.

- Appoint plan ambassadors to help keep employees motivated.
- Create An Ongoing Communications Program: Emails, Newsletter, Professional Advisors, Board Material, and Lifetime Statements.
- Use Qualified Financial Advisors.
- Control Plan Fees.

THE DECISION

In the Tao Te Ching, the Chinese philosopher Laozi (also known as Lao Tzu) wrote that, "The journey of a thousand miles begins with a single step."

While Lao Tzu's actual words have been adapted to today's verbal lexicon, his meaning is as fresh and valid as it was 2500 years ago. The father of Taoism understood that goal achievement, even goals that will take great time, begin with the decision to achieve the goal. The first step.

The term, Tao, means "way," "path," or "principal." It is the journey. Retirement is a journey that begins with a single deposit — or an employer choice.

THE RETIREMENT JOURNEY

If you are in charge of your company's 401(k) plan, meaningful and positive change cannot occur until you make the decision to create improvements. You cannot commit to achieving those improvements until you believe they are possible.

IS IT POSSIBLE?

If you are like many plan sponsors, you are confident that you have done everything possible to encourage employee participation in your plan. You have conducted enrollment meetings. You may have a company match. Your plan has a robust website, and you send a monthly newsletter. You are either pleased or displeased with your results. Perhaps you have accepted the status quo.

No Status Quo

Here is the problem with the status quo: **For most employees, it won't get the job done.**

You have a choice to make. Are you going to accept the status quo? Or, are you willing to take a leap of faith and take the first steps of a new journey for your company?

Are you willing to believe that you can make dramatic improvements to your retirement plan?

DRAMATIC IMPROVEMENTS ARE POSSIBLE

In working with hundreds of companies, it is the author's experience that most companies can significantly enhance employee participation and improve employee investment returns. This statement is backed by facts.

The following is an example of how a single plan design change can improve employee participation.

The following study was funded by The National Institute on Aging, the MacArthur Foundation, the Sloan Foundation, and a National Science Foundation Graduate Research Fellowship. In this study, James J. Choi, et al. conducted a detailed participation and investment analysis, as three companies integrated an ***automatic enrollment feature*** into their existing 401(k) plans.

All employees were now, for the first time, automatically enrolled in the three large plans that were studied. Employees could choose to opt out of the plans if they didn't want to participate.

This single change was able to essentially *double* plan participation.

A summary of the study can be found at the National Bureau of Economic Research._

http://www.nber.org/bah/fall02/401kSaving.html.

After this study, professor Choi and his colleagues noted the following:

"We find that automatic enrollment has a dramatic impact on participation rates. Under automatic enrollment, 401(k) participation rates exceed 85% in all three companies regardless of the tenure of the employee. Prior to automatic enrollment, 401(k) participation rates ranged from 26-43% after six months of tenure at these three firms, and from 57-69% after three years of tenure.

"We also find that automatic enrollment has a large impact on contribution rates and asset allocation choices. Under automatic enrollment, 65-87% of new plan participants save at the default contribution rate and invest exclusively in the default fund. This percentage declines slowly over time, falling to 40-54% after two years of tenure, and to about 45% after three years of tenure (in the two companies for which data extends this far).

"Thus, while automatic enrollment encourages 401(k) participation, it at least temporarily anchors participants at a low savings rate and in a conservative investment vehicle. Higher participation rates raise average wealth accumulation, but a low default savings rate and a conservative default investment undercut accumulation."

For these three companies, a single plan design modification was able to radically change employee participation in their plans.

Was it perfect? No. What is? Employees tended to remain where they were placed, and didn't make improvements. This is a good example of human inertia at work. But it was a start, a good one.

Employee participation grew to nearly 100%. This is a life-changing event for a workforce.

The three studied companies made it *easier to be in* their plans than it was to opt out. This simple plan adjustment allowed *human nature* to change the financial lives of company employees. Prior to the adjustment, nearly half of the company employees were non-participants. They wanted to save for retirement, but their internal chemistry worked against them. Automatic enrollment made an accommodation to human nature, and helped many more employees accomplish their financial goals.

You may be wondering if employees are angered by being automatically enrolled. Studies show that automatic enrollment does not anger employees. It actually *improves* total employee satisfaction in a plan.

ANCHORING

The Choi study noted that plan participants tended to become "anchored" in the default deferral and the default investment choice.

If employees were enrolled at a 3% deferral rate, employees tended to stay there. They often remained in the default investment choice as well.

We have already discussed why anchoring happens. Human nature.

Our internal chemistry is not optimal for retirement investing.

But human nature *can* be managed. We will discuss how to adjust for it when we review plan investment architecture.

The Choi study demonstrates how a simple structural change can improve 401(k) plan participation and satisfaction.

Automatic enrollment is just one of the strategies that plan sponsors can employ to enhance participation and employee wealth accumulation.

The following pages will review other plan strategies for you to consider. Perhaps some of these enhancements will work for your plan.

The journey begins with a single step—the decision to improve your plan. Start now.

ENROLLMENT ARCHITECTURE

Make It Automatic

Every 401(k) program should consider enrolling participants automatically. This feature leads to higher employee participation. Higher participation leads to greater wealth accumulation. Wealth accumulation leads to greater employee appreciation for a plan. This leads to greater productivity.

Note: If your company has high employee turnover, this option may be less attractive, due to administrative expenses. Then again, perhaps it can help reduce employee turnover, and cut hiring costs.

There was a time when automatic enrollment was considered risky for employers to implement. Employers worried that employees would object to being "forced" to save, even though they could easily opt out of a plan. Employers worried that employees would sue plan trustees, for investment losses, or claim discrimination against those who were earning lower incomes.

The first company to implement this type of strategy was fast food chain, McDonald's Corp.

McDonald's had difficulty getting restaurant workers (who earned marginal wages) to participate in their 401(k) plan. Low participation among the less-highly-paid workers forced highly-paid employees to limit their contributions. McDonald's also had high employee turnover.

Automatic enrollment was a natural strategy to reduce turnover and increase plan participation. McDonald's took the risk of adding an automatic enrollment feature to their 401(k). It worked.

Soon, other companies began to add the feature, especially employers paying marginal wages. 7/11 was close behind. As time passed, the IRS issued helpful regulations, at first protecting employers who added this feature, and eventually promoting the idea to businesses and their employees. Here is a link to the IRS page explaining the feature:

http://www.irs.gov/Retirement-Plans/Plan-Participant,-Employee/Retirement-Topics-Automatic-Enrollment

The Department of Labor also has an explanation page, which can be found here:

http://www.dol.gov/ebsa/publications/automaticenrollment-401kplans.html

WHERE TO PUT EMPLOYEE MONEY

Qualified Default Investment Alternative

When an employee becomes automatically enrolled, but does not choose investment options (remember human nature), employers have to put the money somewhere. This is often called the *default investment option*, or Qualified Default Investment Alternative (QDIA).

In the early years of automatic enrollment, companies chose the least risky investment as the default option. Imagine withholding an employee's wages, without active consent, and then losing some of it in the stock market?

The problem with this "safe" option was that the money couldn't grow to outpace inflation. Since one third of employees never choose an investment option, the "safe" investment choice acts more like a savings account than a retirement account. This is better than nothing, but not optimal for retirement accumulation.

With input from many employers and plan participants, the U.S. Department of Labor acted to protect employers and employees, by issuing guidelines that encourage companies to choose a *balanced account*, or appropriate *age-based* asset allocation model as the default investment option.

In October of 2007, the Department of Labor issued its final rule on the default investment option. The following is a quote from document **29 CFR Part 2550** that describes the rule.

"…Section 624(a) of the Pension Protection Act directed that such regulations provide guidance on the appropriateness of designating default investments that include a mix of asset classes consistent with capital preservation or long-term capital appreciation, or a blend of both. In the Department's view, this statutory language provides the stated relief to fiduciaries of any participant directed individual account plan that complies with its terms and with those of the Department's regulation under section 404(c)(5) of ERISA…."

The full DOL document and summary can be read here:

http://www.dol.gov/ebsa/newsroom/fsqdia.html

https://www.dol.gov/.../07-5147.pdf

THE RIGHT CHOICE

A balanced, or target model, will give employee accounts a better opportunity to grow over time. If the QDIA is an appropriate balanced account or model, employers and trustees are protected against employee lawsuits, even if the markets fare poorly.

EMPLOYEES LIKE AUTOMATIC ENROLLMENT

If your 401(k) plan does not utilize automatic enrollment, you may wonder how employees might react to the change. In 2007, Harris Interactive conducted a poll for FINRA, AARP and the Retirement Security Project. Harris polled 10,130 adults, of which 696 were automatically enrolled in their 401(k) and 48 who had opted out. Harris found that 97% of those who were automatically enrolled, and remained in the plan, were satisfied with the plan. 90% of those who opted out were satisfied with the plan. 95% of the plan participants felt that automatic enrollment made saving for retirement easy. What's to lose?

WHAT PERCENTAGE?

6% Default Target

The traditional automatic enrollment default percentage for 401(k) plans has been 3%.

3% deferrals are not nearly enough to prepare employees for retirement. You should consider choosing an automatic deferral percentage of 6%.

John Beshears, James Choi, et al, (2009) demonstrated that there is *no significant difference* in employee drop-out rates when the automatic enrollment amount is increased to 6% from 3%. Approximately 10% of automatic enrollees will opt out, whether the default is 3% or 6%.

Government regulatory protections allow an automatic deferral of 6%. You should consider it seriously.

Most people need to save between 10% and 15% of their pay to achieve financial independence in retirement. With an initial deferral rate of 6%, employees will be deferring about half of what they need for retirement.

Your employees deserve the best chance for retirement security. If you are not helping them with automatic deferrals of 6%, this is something you should seriously consider.

This book shows you how to help employees save even more— hopefully enough for them to achieve their retirement dreams.

RE-ENROLL YOUR OPT-OUTS

Financial circumstances change. People get married and divorced. Employees have children and plan for college expenses. They buy homes and cars. They pay off loans. Their spouses go to work. They earn raises or get second jobs. Nothing stays the same.

Employers cannot assume that someone who opted out of their plan in the past doesn't want to save today.

- Some employees experience "non-enrollment remorse," wishing they had never opted out of a plan in the first place.

- Some employees find that another year closer to retirement causes stress, which makes them embrace a new chance to save.

- Others simply won't have the will to fight inertia a second time, and allow their automatic retirement savings (wealth accumulation) to happen for them.

Never assume that employees want financial failure. They want financial freedom. Re-enrollment can help more employees save into your plan, and they will thank you for it.

Financial security (saving for retirement) is important. It is near the top of everyone's wish list, and at the base of the need pyramid. Sometimes, circumstances cause a delay in savings. Sometimes, employees make poor financial choices that they would like to correct. Give them the chance.

When

The start of each year is a good time to re-enroll non-participating employees, even if they have opted out in the past.

Employees will be able to opt out of your plan, as before. A surprising number of employees may choose to remain enrolled the second time around.

EASY ENROLL

Yes or No

If you can't bring yourself to implement automatic enrollment, an easy-enrollment architecture should be installed.

The easier it is to enroll in a plan, the higher the participation. If all employees must do is check a box labeled "yes" to enroll, they will be more inclined to participate. Employees should be given this choice immediately after viewing the enrollment (education and features) presentation for your plan. This is when their motivation to save will be the greatest.

With an Easy Enroll feature, employees can choose an automatic deferral amount. Employees can be automatically placed into an age-based or balanced asset allocation model.

At some point, employees should fill out the important paperwork, such as their investment options and a beneficiary designation. But this does not need to be done prior to an employee's enrollment in a plan.

If an employee has to wade through a mound of documents, such as education materials thick enough to serve as a doorstop, they might set their enrollment paperwork aside for a mythical "later," a time that never comes. Make it easy.

When you make it simple for employees to enroll, they will find it easier to overcome the stress of paperwork, and the stress of making choices. They **will** participate.

Chapter Thirty-Nine
R
The Company Match

THE COMPANY MATCH

If you own a company, or help administer a 401(k) plan, you should understand how a company match will influence employee deferrals.

A company match creates incentive for employees to participate. A minimum match can also qualify a plan for reduced regulatory compliance administration.

The Plan Sponsor Council of America (PSCA) conducts an annual survey report, which compiles retirement plan data, such as average company contributions and participation rates.

The PSCA report states that the most common matching formula (by far) is 50% of the first 6% of pay. This may be a waste of company money.

HOW MUCH IMPACT?

In 2010, the U.S. Bureau of Labor Statistics compiled extensive national data on the effect of retirement plan matching in their National Compensation Survey (NCS). After detailed analysis, this study determined that a company match had less impact than expected. A company match could be attributed to as much as a 12.9% increase in employee plan participation, or as little as 2.8%.

MATCH VERSUS AUTOMATIC ENROLLMENT

Automatic enrollment provisions are associated with up to an 11% jump in plan participation, increasing over time. Some statistical analysis put the plan participation increase due to automatic enrollment as low as 8%.

According to the Bureau of Labor Report, *automatic enrollment can be just as effective as a company match in driving plan participation.* Combined, they produce a win for all.

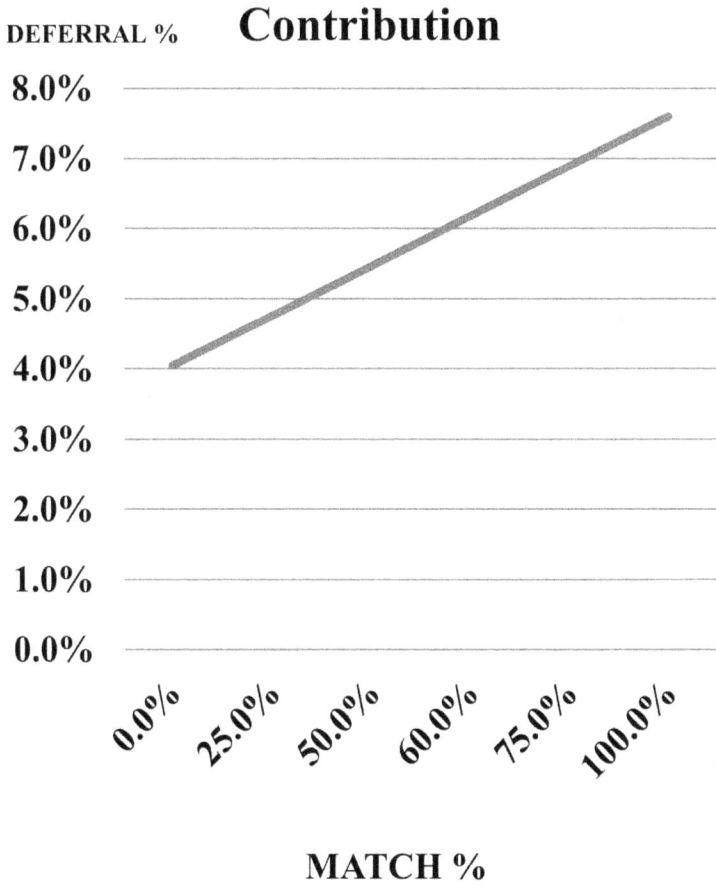

Matching Elasticity

Deferral Vs. Match % Contribution

In economics, there is a term called elasticity. Elasticity measures responsiveness, the change in one axis (X) relative to changes in another (Y).

If the price for a gallon of gasoline rises by one percent, there will be a small reduction in the amount of gasoline purchased. Demand, at minor price increases, is inelastic — it changes little.

The demand curve for gasoline changes as prices change. When gasoline gets a little more expensive, we buy a tiny bit less. When gasoline prices double, we find other uses for our money. Consumption drops more rapidly. We carpool, we work from home, and we travel less.

As prices rise significantly, demand begins to fall more rapidly. Demand, at much high prices, has greater elasticity.

Gasoline is considered an "essential." Most people must buy gas, regardless of price. For "non-essential" items, the demand curve can be far more elastic. A rapid, and sustained, doubling of movie theater (or restaurant dinner) prices might nearly kill the industry.

401(K) ELASTICITY

The responsiveness to 401(k) matching contributions has a measurable, and somewhat predictable, elasticity. This allows us to quantify the *effectiveness* of a company match.

According to a study published by the National Bureau of Economics (Engelhardt & Kumar), the relative elasticity of a 401(k) match is between 0.15 and 0.27. For example: When a company match is increased from *50% on the first six percent* to *100% on the first six percent* (a 100% change), employees will increase their contributions into the plan by about *25%*.

Elasticity remains fairly constant as the match extends to higher deferral percentages.

According to the U.S. Bureau of Labor Statistics, "Using administrative data from Watson Wyatt, Clark and Schieber (1998) find that employees receiving a 50-75 percent match are 28 percentage points more likely to participate than employees receiving a 25 percent match."

Using data from the Health and Retirement Survey, Cunningham and Engelhardt (2002) estimate that (unconditional) employee contribution percentages increased by just *19 percent* of the employer matches observed in their sample.

WHAT ELASTICITY MEANS FOR MATCHING

There is a substantial body of statistical data that predicts the *effect* of a company match on employee contribution levels. A company match *will* increase participation, but *not* by as much as most employers think. Why do it, then?

Companies have better participation with a match than without one. Companies want to encourage employees to save, and they want to help them plan for retirement. They also want to help top executives save more.

The average amount that highly paid employees can defer into a plan is limited by the average deferral percentage participation of the less highly compensated employees. A match raises the deferral limits for management and ownership.

LET'S GET OPTIMAL

A better understanding of the economics of matching will lead some employers to seek a *more optimal use* of company funds. This chart shows employee deferrals with a 50% match to 6%

of pay.

Example:
50% Matching To 6%

Deferral Vs. Match

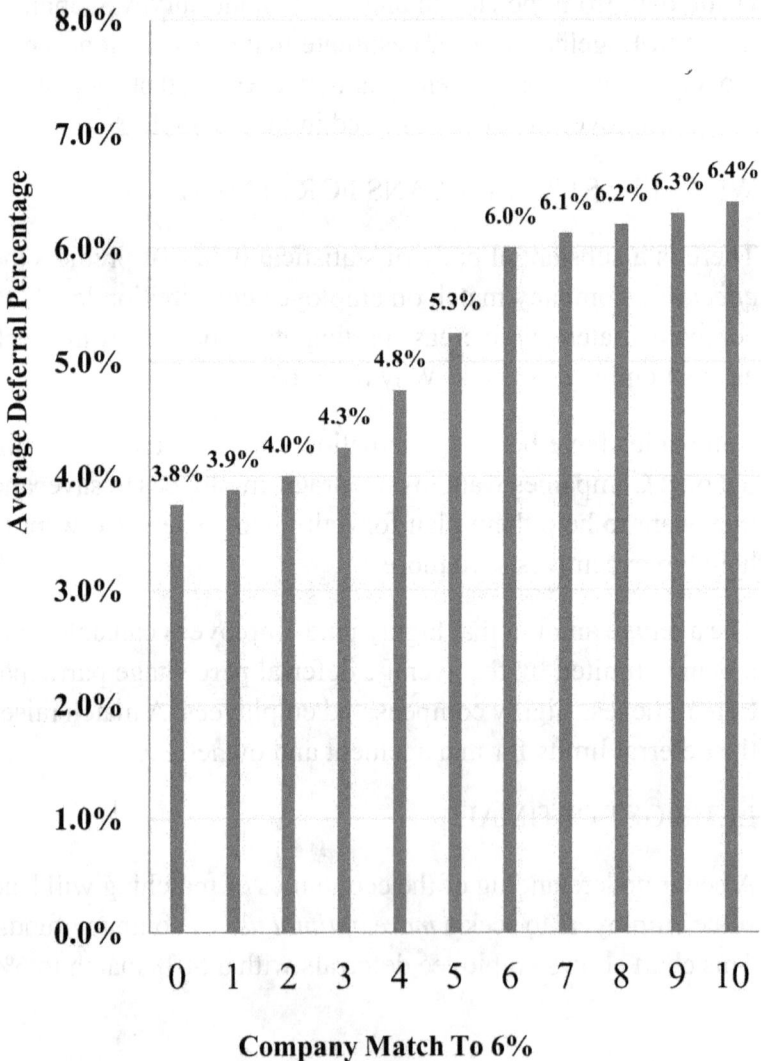

Chart: Average Deferral Percentage vs. Company Match To 6%

Company Match To 6%	Average Deferral Percentage
0	3.8%
1	3.9%
2	4.0%
3	4.3%
4	4.8%
5	5.3%
6	6.0%
7	6.1%
8	6.2%
9	6.3%
10	6.4%

A MATCHING STRATEGY FOR OPTIMAL EMPLOYEE PARTICIPATION

When thinking "bang for the buck," employers should consider the *marginal utility* (elasticity) of the employer match.

COMPARATIVE EXAMPLE

Because of the consistent elasticity, a match of *25% on the first 10%* of deferrals (2.5% overall) can be *more effective* at enhancing overall deferral percentages than *50% on the first 6%* (3% overall). Employees may do more with lower total match.

Do More With Less

If your goal is to have high participation and a high deferral percentage,...if your goal is to encourage employees to save more for retirement...the optimum matching strategy might be a *lower* percentage match to a *higher* deferral amount.

Let's say your company has a 50% match on the first 6%. You might increase employee deferrals significantly by changing to a 30% match on the first 10%.

This change yields the same maximum *net amount* of match for each employee. But it creates *incentive* for employees to save ten percent, rather than six percent, to receive all the free company money.

The following chart shows deferral percentages when the match is stretched to 10% from 6%.

Example:
30% Matching To 10%

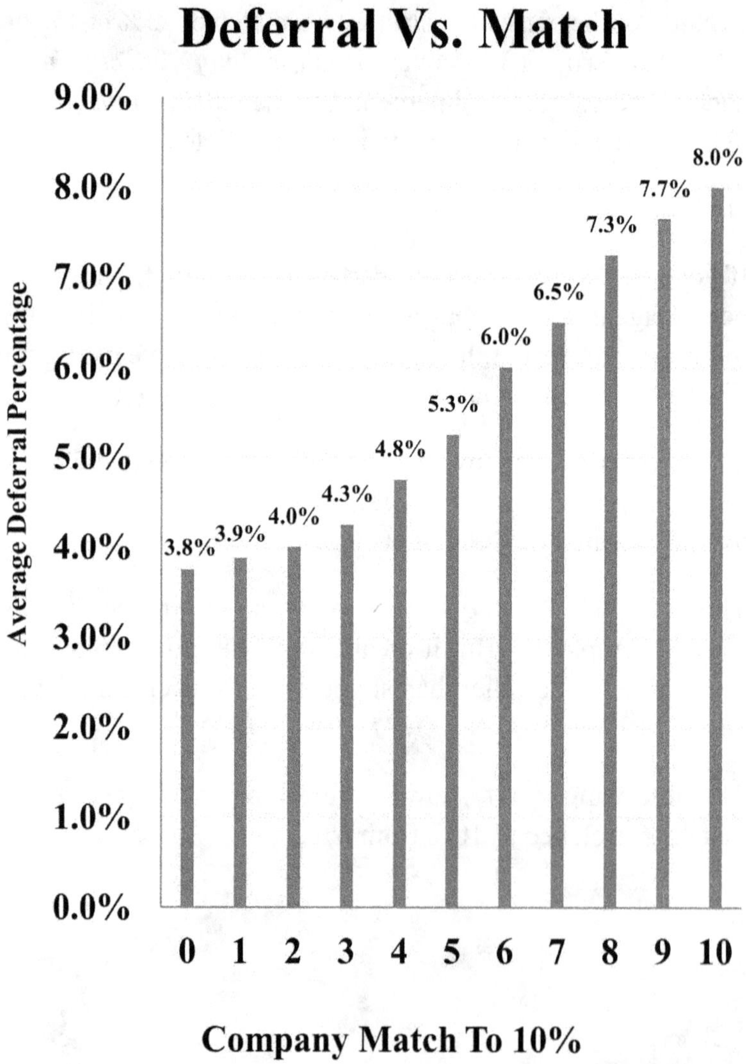
Deferral Vs. Match
9.0%
8.0%
7.0%
6.0%
5.0%
4.0%
3.0%
2.0%
1.0%
0.0%
Average Deferral Percentage
3.8%
3.9%
4.0%
4.3%
4.8%
5.3%
6.0%
6.5%
7.3%
7.7%
8.0%
0
1
2
3
4
5
6
7
8
9
10
Company Match To 10%

STRETCHED OUT

With a stretched matching design, an employee receiving 30% on 10% will get the same company contribution as they would with 50% on 6%. If employees want the full company match, they will need to *work* for it by saving more for themselves.

A 30% match, versus a 50% match does *not* create a disincentive to save. It creates more incentive. Employees take "free money" as readily as before. Yet, stretching the match to 10% of deferrals will cause employees to save more of their own funds.

In this example, average employee deferrals have risen from 6.4% (when using 50% of the first 6%) to a full 8% (with 30% of the first 10%).

This gets the plan closer to its goal of a 10% average deferral—the minimum that employees will need to achieve financial security in retirement.

IMPORTANT NOTE

Not all employees will defer to 10%. This may allow an employer to offer a match closer to 40% of the first 10%, with the same company outlay as 50% of the first 6%. This strategy will create a strong incentive to increase overall plan participation. It may also help the best savers (often senior management) earn an even higher company match than before. Note: Make sure that this does not create problems with your plan's Average Contribution Percentage (ACP) testing limits.

The following chart shows the effect of combining a stretched match with an Auto-Enroll feature in a plan.

Example: 30% Matching To 10% With 25% Increase From Auto Enroll

Deferral Vs. Match

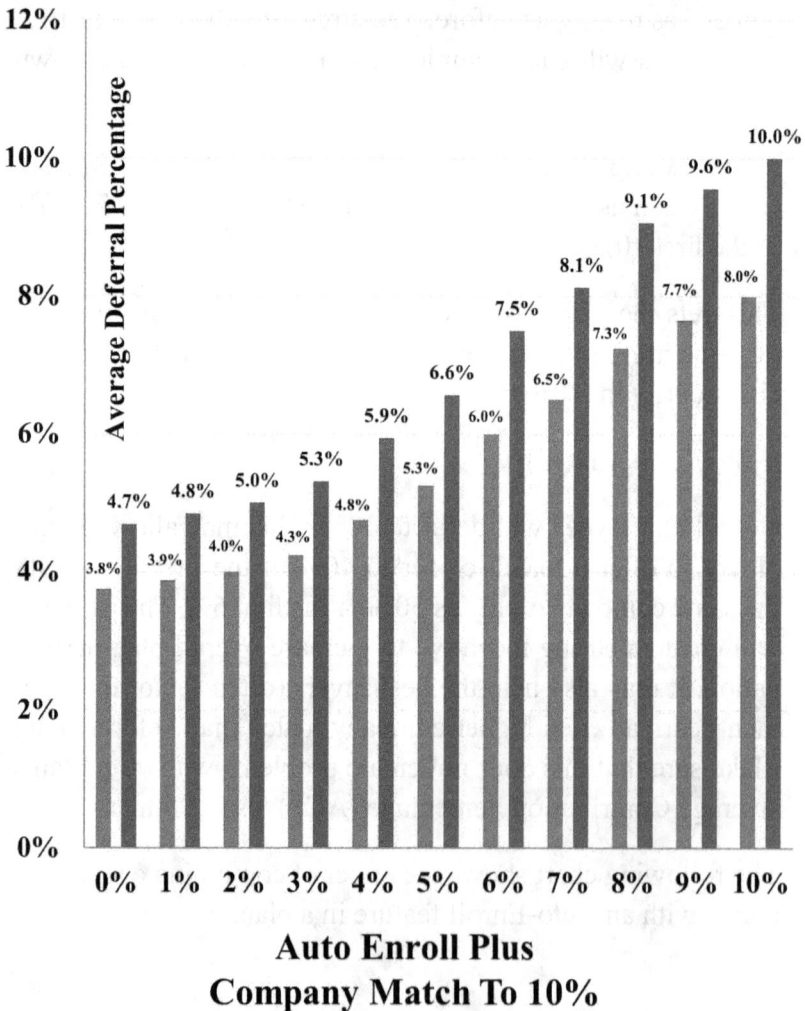

Average Deferral Percentage (y-axis)

Auto Enroll Plus Company Match To 10%	Series 1	Series 2
0%	3.8%	4.7%
1%	3.9%	4.8%
2%	4.0%	5.0%
3%	4.3%	5.3%
4%	4.8%	5.9%
5%	5.3%	6.6%
6%	6.0%	7.5%
7%	6.5%	8.1%
8%	7.3%	9.1%
9%	7.7%	9.6%
10%	8.0%	10.0%

Auto Enroll Plus Company Match To 10%

STRETCHED MATCH PLUS AUTO ENROLL

When an extended matching formula is combined with an automatic enrollment feature, employee participation should be greatly enhanced. Since most employees would like to save more for retirement, this strategy is embraced by employees as a highly workable and welcome solution to their participation dilemma.

Combining a 30% match, up to a 10% salary deferral, with automatic enrollment boosts our sample average employee deferrals from 8% to 10%.

MATCH OPTIMIZATION VERSUS SAFE HARBOR

When an employer changes a 401(k) matching strategy to encourage higher employee savings, it may move a plan out of the safe harbor zone for compliance testing. Care must be taken to ensure that a decent number of the less-highly compensated group of employees remain in the plan. Small companies have a higher risk of unbalancing contributions if they opt out of a safe harbor match.

The National Institute on Aging funded a study by Brigitte Madrian and Dennis Shea. (Harvard Quarterly Journal of Economics, November, 2001) This study determined that auto-takeoff increased overall plan participation from 70% to 90%. It also *reduced* the *deferral disparity* between highly compensated and non-highly compensated employees to just 14%. (80% of the non-highly compensated deferred versus 94% of the highly compensated employees) The average deferral among the less highly compensated employees rose to 8%. By ERISA law, this would allow an average deferral percentage for the highly compensated group of 10% (Non-highly average plus 2%). A 10% average for highly compensated employees is often sufficient to let everyone participate as desired.

Talk to your plan advisors to see if stretching your match makes sense for your company.

The next section shows another strategy that can increase employee deferrals even more.

AUTOMATIC DEFERRAL INCREASES

Richard Thaler and Shlomo Benartzi studied the effectiveness of *combining* automatic enrollment with an automatic deferral increase in 401(k) plans (Journal of Political Economy, Vol. 112, No. 1, pp. S164-S187, February 2004). In the three plans studied, an initial minimum automatic deferral was combined with annual automatic deferral increases. The increases occurred at the beginning of each calendar year. 78% joined the auto deferral program. 80% of those employees remained in the program through the fourth deferral raise.

The average savings rates in the studied plans increased from 3.5% to 13.6% over the course of forty months!

This study illustrates how modifications that cater to human nature can increase employee financial security. An average savings rate of 3.5% will not help employees achieve financial security. A 13.6% deferral will help many employees achieve security in retirement.

Congress blessed automatic deferral increases in The Pension Protection Act of 2006, by protecting employers against employee discrimination lawsuits.

Most record keepers have built auto features into their plan documents and administrative architecture. You should discuss these enhancements with your plan advisors, and implement them if you can.

WILL IT WORK FOR YOU?

Some executives have a difficult time imagining how automatic deferral and enrollment features can be successfully implemented with their company 401(k) plan. The facts don't lie. It usually works.

Note: If you are a small company with less than ten employees, a few opt-outs could defeat this strategy. The best way to overcome skeptics is with education. This may involve seminars and face-to-face meetings with a financial advisor.

SUMMARY

Automatic features will help more employees accomplish what they want, but can't do on their own. It helps them achieve financial security. If you feel an obligation to help your company's employees, you're not alone. More and more employers are integrating automatic enrollment and auto increase features into their 401(k) plans.

Be open-minded about these concepts. Do not fall prey to thoughts like, "This can't work for my company." Or, "My employees won't like this." These enhancements work. They are popular with employees. Make this your mindset.

A successful retirement journey for your employees might just begin with a single step, your decision to make this work.

Example: 30% Matching To 10% With Auto Enroll & Auto Increase

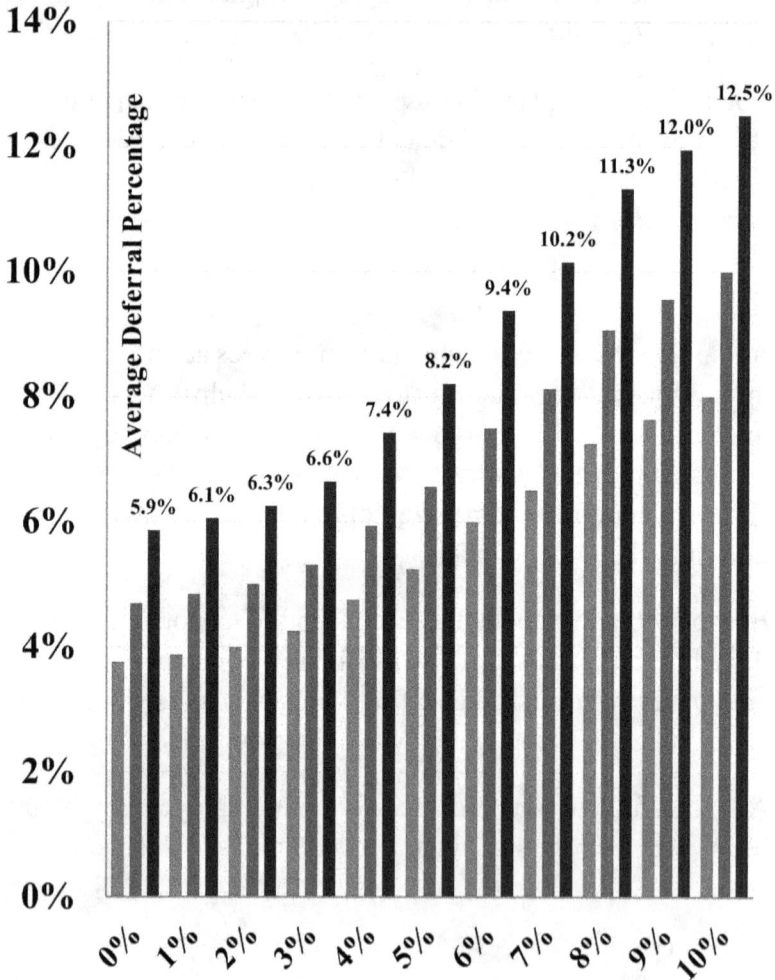

Average Deferral Percentage

Auto Enroll Plus
Company Match To 10%

ALL FEATURES COMBINED

The preceding chart illustrates the results that might be gained from implementing multiple employee participation strategies — auto enroll, auto increase and a stretched match.

The lower percentages represent a company stretching their match to 30% on the first 10% of deferrals.

The middle percentages represent adding automatic enrollment to the stretched match.

The highest set of numbers represents the implementation of a stretched match, automatic enrollment and automatic deferral increases.

The illustrated plan has increased the average deferral percentages from 6.4% (with the 50% match up to 6%) to a full 12.5% of income. These percentages are in line with actual studies, and normal elasticities.

These three, easy to implement changes could have a dramatic impact upon the financial security of your employees.

As wealth increases, employees have less stress. They become more productive workers. They feel better about themselves. They are happier with the plan.

Make your employees happy.

$&¢

Chapter Forty

_____R_____

The Human 401(k)

WHAT IS BEST FOR YOUR PLAN?

Every company would like to improve employee participation in their 401(k) plan. Auto features and a stretched match are effective ways to accomplish this goal.

Perhaps you worry about poor reactions if you make these improvements. Don't. People fear change. People don't like the unknown. This is human nature. We've discussed this.

Changes soon become the new normal.

Once employees have experienced the benefits of auto features, their opinions change. They embrace their growing wealth.

401(K) EVOLUTION

TRADITIONAL 401(K)

The traditional 401(k) was designed by technicians, administrators and investment advisors. The recordkeeping and administration features were designed to work smoothly. Top investments were provided.

Traditional 401(k) designs were not constructed to embrace human behavior. Neuro behaviorists weren't consulted. Industrial economists had nothing to analyze. Plans were elegant in theory, but less effective in execution.

THE HUMAN 401(K)

As academic specialists have worked with plan creators, new techniques have emerged in 401(k) design. You have now learned them. Use them. They work.

Employers can often double employee deferral percentages, simply by making their plans more user-friendly.

If your plan has an average deferral rate below 12%, think about adding enhancements to help more of your employees achieve financial independence. You can make a difference — a life-changing difference.

IMPLEMENTING AUTOMATIC DEFERRALS

If you add auto features, a few employees may grumble at first. Some employees complain about everything. Your match is too low…the investments haven't performed as well as the latest "hot" funds…the website is hard to use… A few employees may opt out of the plan. Many more will stay in.

Auto features are paternalistic, not controlling. They are implemented for employee benefit. There are few valid arguments against them. The DOL encourages auto features.

This strategy succeeds exceptionally well, especially as employee size grows larger. This is due to the law of numbers, where a few opt-outs won't materially affect the average.

Smaller companies must present the key information effectively. They must make the effort to educate, because a few non-takers will affect the outcome.

Once employees understand what's at stake...their realistic financial futures...good things happen. Once an employee calculates their own personal number, they usually opt in favor of financial security, rather than opting out and choosing future poverty.

This book recommends an automatic **deferral floor of 6%**. If you fear how this might be accepted, try a floor of 4%. You can always increase it later.

AUTOMATIC INCREASES

When you combine automatic deferrals with automatic increases, it will take little time for employees to achieve significant deferral percentages. Any employee can reach a 10% deferral rate without lifting a finger, or suffering the angst of paperwork and investment selections.

SET A GOAL

As a company, you should set a plan deferral goal. A good plan goal is to achieve an ***automatic employee deferral rate of 10%.*** This should get your overall plan deferral percentage in the range of 12% or more.

When designing an automatic increase, you should attempt to get your employees to 10% as soon as you can, without having employees opt out of your plan.

If you start with a 4% floor, 2% annual increases will bring an employee's deferral rate to 10% by year four.

If you start with a base of 6%, a 2% annual increase gets an employee to a 10% deferral by year three. A 1% increase accomplishes that goal by year five.

The faster your plan accelerates deferrals, the quicker you will help your employees.

TURNOVER

Every company has turnover. Turnover is a normal part of any business operation. Many companies require a year of employment before employees are eligible to enroll in their 401(k) plan.

If employees leave your company for another, those employees will lose valuable time in achieving their retirement objectives. For many, there will be a year-long wait before being eligible to enroll in their new plans. The new employers may not have automatic enrollment. Your employees may choose low (or no) deferral rates. This will set them back *years* in their retirement planning, or derail them forever.

Help your employees help themselves. They will reward you with higher productivity and long-term loyalty.

POSITIVE FEEDBACK

When employees begin deferring at higher rates, they begin to experience positive feedback. As balances increase, dopamine is released into the body. This motivates. As financial security grows, serotonin is released. This stimulates feelings of well-being. Our neurotransmitters will imprint and solidify a new savings habit. Once experienced, many employees will defer highly for the rest of their working lives—all because you adapted your plan to fit their inner nature.

EMPLOYEE ASSESSMENT

It is easy to assess employee needs and desires with quick surveys. Most plan providers have printed pieces or Internet questionnaires that can help your company implement new strategies. Make sure that your surveys focus on positive employee goals, rather than uninformed negativity. People don't like change. They fear it.

Research demonstrates that employees consistently underestimate their abilities to save. They can — and will — save amounts they thought were impossible, if you help them.

MAKE IT EASIER TO STAY IN THE PLAN THAN TO OPT OUT

We have reviewed ways to enhance participation in your 401(k). By now, you should recognize the success pattern. If you make something easy, employees are prone to accept (or choose) that path. If you make something difficult, even if the difficulty is a minor inconvenience (like naming a beneficiary) some employees avoid it. They will find less stressful things to do, like get a cup of coffee, chit chat, or browse the Internet. They might even do some work.

Employers must allow employees to opt out of a retirement plan, especially if they join the plan through automatic enrollment. While the opt-out process can't be impractical, there is no law against having procedures that bring human inertia into play.

Certain procedures are proven winners when it comes to helping employees remain in a plan:

- Opt-out paperwork will discourage some employees from removing themselves from a plan, especially if those employees have to take certain steps to obtain it.

- It is harder to make a trip to the HR office to pick up paperwork, than it is to have it delivered to a computer inbox. Make your employees effort themselves, like walking to your office, to obtain their opt-out documents.

- It is harder to schedule a plan exit meeting than it is to pick up the phone or send an email to un-enroll. You might ask employees to meet with a company representative, or speak with an outside plan consultant, to discuss options that don't involve total removal from a plan. It is easy to persuade employees to save for themselves. Employees want to save, and they can. Sometimes, they just don't think they can, until they do.

- As an employee fills out an "exit questionnaire," she might think twice about sabotaging a secure retirement future. Your questionnaire may explain the risks of not planning for retirement. It can provide relevant facts that encourage saving behavior (such as the education companion to this book).

If you make employees work harder to opt out of a plan, rather than remain in, sometimes their natural instincts take over and work in their favor.

Chapter Forty-One

R

Simplify Your Plan

SIMPLIFY YOUR PLAN

401(k)s have evolved substantially since they were first created. In the early 1980s, 401(k)s were limited in investment choices. Early plans had only two or three investment choices—a stock account, a bond account, and maybe a fixed account. Most plans were offered through insurance companies, with the investments inside an annuity contract. Mutual fund companies offered plans with their funds only.

Section 404(c) of the Internal Revenue Code encouraged changes in the fiduciary behavior by plan sponsors. 404(c) changed 401(k) plan architecture by waiving fiduciary liability for investment losses if the guidelines were followed.

The 404(c) guidelines included a minimum of *three* investment account types that had to be offered in every plan. This guideline (regulation) remains in effect today. In 2007, Section 404(c) was modified to encourage the use of a balanced account for the default investment if none is chosen by employees.

In the 1990s, *open architecture* allowed a (virtually) limitless array of investment choices to be offered in a 401(k) plan. This is still the "gold standard" of investment design. Open architecture has limitations, especially when there are *too many* investment choices.

FEE DISCLOSURE

In 2012, the Department of Labor issued regulations that affect the *disclosure requirements* of 401(k) plan fiduciaries. These regulations expanded the required deliverance of detailed information regarding *plan fees.* This includes both direct and indirect fees.

MAKE IT SIMPLE—AND BRILLIANT

According to Dalbar, Inc.'s 2015 QAIB survey, the 20-year average investor return in equities was 5.19%. The average return of the S&P 500 during that time was 9.8%. This is a difference of 4.61%. Equity investors earned 88% *less* than their target index. Such an investment disparity would be devastating for anyone seeking to retire with financial security. Morningstar, Inc. has found similar statistics in their own studies.

The education companion to this book illustrates how poorly the average equity investor fares against simple, passive stock indexes. This return disparity is destructive. It occurs because investors allow themselves to be ruled by emotions. Investors buy high and sell low. This is not ideal.

Age-based and *asset allocation models* remove emotions from employee investment decisions. Employees rarely move out of models. This allows employees to achieve higher overall returns than those who jump in and out of various asset classes, based upon what's in the news.

NEW TREND—Narrow The Options

For three decades, plan providers sought to expand employee choice in plan investments. Employers offered larger and larger fund menus, including individual brokerage accounts that allowed participants to trade many securities, almost at will.

The current seismic trend in 401(k) investment design is to *limit* the number of investment choices, not expand them. Large companies are channeling employees into asset allocation, or age-based models, rather than presenting large individual fund menus.

RULES OF BEHAVIOR

Behavioral studies show that plan participation falls as the number of investment choices grows. Sheena Iyengar, et al., 2004 demonstrated that, for every ten choices offered, enrollment drops 1.5% to 2%. When a plan gets confusing, some employees withdraw.

MODEL PLANS

More and more 401(k)s are offering a mix of aged-based, or asset allocation models, with just a limited number of mutual funds to aid personalization by asset class.

For example, a company plan might offer four or five model accounts. Another five or six managed or indexed mutual funds might round out the mix. The funds usually represent major investment classes—such as large stocks, small stocks, international stocks, bonds, Treasury Inflation-Protected Securities or a money market fund.

Ten to fourteen plan choices should be enough to allow for investment diversification, without sacrificing overall employee investment performance.

AUTOMATIC INVESTMENT

Automatic enrollment can improve employee plan deferrals and employee wealth accumulation.

Similar benefits can be achieved by *automatically enrolling* participants into *aged-based* asset allocation models. Plans can be designed to *automatically adjust* between models as employees grow older.

Because of inertia, we know that 80%-90% of employees will remain where they are placed. If history is any guide to the future, we know that these models will improve employee investment returns.

The Morningstar and Dalbar studies predict how well average investors might fare in models, rather than managing their own investment selections. Models don't let employee emotions sabotage a long-term investment plan. It is a winning strategy.

INFORMATION ARCHITECTURE

Changing a plan's structural architecture, to include auto-enroll, auto-increase, and a stretched match can improve plan participation. Some of these enhancements are subtle. Others require more effort and explanation. All of them work.

Changing a plan's investment *information architecture* can also help employees. This does not mean increasing the volume of investment education. It usually means changing how information is delivered. Sometimes less is more.

Most 401(k) plans offer more investment information than employees will read in a lifetime. This can cause some employees to store it away for later. Sometimes, it gets put in a file with their enrollment paperwork, and never sees daylight again.

While detailed investment materials are required under ERISA, they don't always help employees understand what they need to know. They don't awaken the emotions that employees need to invest for security.

Meaningful education must elicit the *emotions* that employees must *feel* before they take meaningful action.

The education companion to this book, *Making Cent$ of Investing*, delivers education in a way that prompts action. Some of the information is distressing. But it is the truth.

When the right education material is presented to employees, they develop a greater understanding of what retirement will look like without proper planning. They feel more motivated to build a roadmap to their goals. They become compelled to act.

Proper education can change an employee's mindset from passive to active (fixed mindset to growth mindset). When effective education is combined with user-friendly structural changes, employee participation will rise dramatically.

$&¢

Chapter Forty-Two

R

Face The Facts

WHAT'S IN A FACE?

Our brains are hard-wired to think in certain ways. But our brains have some neuroplasticity. This allows for behavioral adaptation.

The challenge is this: How can we create more positive savings and investment behavior, given our brain chemistry?

Hal Hershfield earned his Ph.D. in psychology from Stanford University. For his doctoral thesis, Hershfield studied the role that time horizons play on our emotional experience and decision making. Dr. Hershfield conducted his studies by using functional MRIs to map brain electrical activity, specifically in the frontal section of the cerebral cortex.

http://www.ncbi.nlm.nih.gov/pmc/articles/PMC3764505/

https://hbr.org/2013/06/you-make-better-decisions-if-you-see-your-senior-self

Professor Hershfield found that different areas of the brain become stimulated when we think about ourselves, versus when we think about strangers.

Hershfield's subjects were also asked to imagine themselves in the future. When they did, their brain stimulation patterns were more similar to the "stranger" pattern, than they were to those of themselves. When we picture our own, personal future self, our brain can see this as *someone else*.

FUTURE DISCONNECTION

Some people are more connected to their *future* selves than others. Some of us find it more difficult to envision ourselves living years from now. It's just how our brains work. This makes it more difficult to participate in a 401(k).

Hershfield's research helped answer the question of why some people find it harder to save for the future than others. Some brains are naturally wired to see a future self as *someone else*. Why sacrifice today for someone else in the future?

401(k) education must find a way to overcome this natural limitation in how some people think.

This book has already shown how thoughts and emotions drive investment behavior. Hershfield's research provides another example of how 401(k) plan education can be adapted to human nature.

Hershfield continued his studies with Dan Goldstein and William Sharpe, a Nobel laureate.

Hershfield, Goldstein and Sharpe (Hershfield, et al., 2011) created a virtual reality, with lifelike, personalized avatars. Their research found that avatars are able to alter our perceptions, and influence individual behaviors.

Stanford students were asked to take part in an experiment. One group was asked to view aged pictures of their "personal avatars". Another group did not. The two groups were then asked to create hypothetical retirement savings plans. The students who had seen their personal avatars aged into the future elected to save 30% more than those who didn't.

Hershfield's creative research illustrates just one other way that a 401(k) can be modified to adjust to normal human behavior, and individual needs.

FACIAL AGING APPS

Facial aging applications can be downloaded to any phone, tablet or computer. Facial aging tools can take an employee's picture and render a future "self" image twenty, thirty or forty years in the future.

Facial aging is an unusual, but effective 401(k) educational tool. Aging apps, such as Aging Booth, can be found in such places as the Apple Store and Google Play.

With this application, employees can "see" how *they* might look when they reach retirement age—just like Hershfield's Stanford students. As employees plan for their retirement, they can view their own face, not that of a stranger. This can help them save even more, by stimulating the proper region of their brains.

HAPPY FACE IN A HAPPY PLACE

Can you imagine increasing plan deferrals by 30%, just by helping your employees see their actual selves projected into the future?

Have each of your employees take a smiling, "happy" photo of their own face, and then age it to retirement. This "retirement face" will help employees trigger the appropriate brain patterns they need to see *themselves* in retirement, rather than the face of some stranger.

SIMPLIFY FOR HUMAN NATURE

Higher 401(k) plan participation results from building a *human* plan, rather than a *technical* plan. Here is an example of technical versus a human.

Imagine this: You are having problems with an older computer. You pay $30 for technical support, and get it from someone sitting halfway around the world. Technical support (notice that this is not called human support) tells you that, "you have an APIC problem. You have poor interrupt routing efficiency in your multiprocessor..."

You ask what that means, and you hear this, "...Your system bus isn't engaging properly..."

You hang up the phone.

What you needed to hear was, "Your computer won't work? I'm sorry. No problem. Restart it and the problem should fix itself..."

Most plan participants don't care that a fund's "Sharpe Ratio is high and its R Squared is low..." Participants prefer to hear, "This fund model is built for someone your age. It seeks to maximize gain over time, without taking extra risk..."

Plan fiduciaries must be concerned with alpha, beta, Sharpe ratios and R-squared. But this information does not need to be the focus of employee education. Employees will just get confused. Make things easy.

SUMMARY

You have learned many ways to adapt your 401(k) plan to how people behave. Now, you can take the first step to helping your employees make that long retirement journey.

Chapter Forty-Three

R

Marketing Your Plan To Employees

MARKET YOUR PLAN

Okay. You've decided to shape your retirement plan to conform to the needs of real people. Now, you must implement the changes effectively.

A 401(k) plan must be properly *marketed* to employees, just like the products or services that are provided by any company. Without proper marketing, the sales of any product (employee participation) will lag.

401(k) marketing exists in many forms. Your marketing plan should use multiple strategies to deliver your message. Here are a few ideas.

Enrollment

- Think of your 401(k) enrollment presentation as a *sales* presentation. Your enrollment presentation should present your product (plan) in the best manner possible. It should *compel* positive action. For example: *Making Cent$ of Investing* gives examples of why employees must save, and the results employees might expect.

- Remember this. Your plan is *competing* for employee dollars. Employees will find other uses for their funds if they are not sold on saving for themselves. Your enrollment presentation must provide a persuasive argument that convinces employees to plan for their retirement, rather than waste their money on other things today. Your presentation can't be a simple list of boring plan features. It must sell the benefits. It must elicit emotions. It must sizzle. Make it count.

Drip Marketing

- If you have ever studied marketing, you are aware that the repeated mention of a product or service makes prospects more susceptible to choosing that product. You can create your own drip campaign, with emails and communications of your own. This might include links to appropriate articles that help educate employees about relevant topics. Don't overuse this technique to the point where employees tune it out. But do remind them of the benefits of saving for retirement.

Advertising

- Advertising works. Advertising drives consumers to products. It also helps keep existing customers. Posters, newsletters and internal web postings are effective strategies to advertise your retirement plan. The more you keep your plan in employee consciousness, the more employees will like the plan, and the more they will participate.

Testimonials

- One of the most powerful forms of marketing is personal testimonials. Whether a testimonial is from a recognizable celebrity, or a participating employee endorsing your plan, the results can be equally effective. Goodwill ambassadors can be as effective as any Hollywood star. And you don't have to pay them.

- You should have at least one employee on your Investment Policy Committee. Look for someone who is quietly respected by your rank and file. This does *not* mean that you should choose one of your most vocal employees, or someone who is "sure" that they know more about investing than anyone else. Look for the quiet leader, not the boisterous know-it-all.

- Your plan ambassador should become knowledgeable about your plan's education materials. Your ambassador should be informed about the plan itself. If you have a larger company, you may enlist the help of multiple plan ambassadors. Remember: These people are NOT trained investment professionals. They should not be giving specific investment advice. They should know how to direct employees to your education materials and to your plan's investment experts.

Real Employee Stories

- True employee stories can help shape the opinions of others. Let's say that you employ someone who is not highly paid, but has been deferring into your company's retirement plan for years. You have an employee making $30,000 per year who has been deferring 10% into your plan for a decade. This employee's deferrals have totaled $24,000, with a total company match total of $6,000. With growth, perhaps this employee now has $60,000 in your plan. Ask your plan's investment advisors to help you prepare a compliant graphic to be included (with anonymity and permission) of this example and use it in your company presentation, a newsletter or an email. You can also "project" this employee's account at retirement time, showing a more significant investment balance.

- The same might be done to contrast the account growth of various investment style options. For example: A "safe" investor with similar deposits may have accumulated only $40,000 in the same decade.

- You can also create hypothetical employee examples using your funds' historical returns.

- Show the power of choosing asset allocation models rather than the safest, short-term investment choices.

CONSISTENCY OF MESSAGE

A successful marketing plan should be consistent and ongoing. Never stop reminding employees how their plan is built for them and why they should use it and use it often.

Chapter Forty-Four

_____R_____

Lifetime Statements & Lifetime Planning

LIFETIME STATEMENTS

Quarterly statements are mandated by ERISA regulations. The traditional quarterly statement gives a snapshot summary of deposits and investment returns for the prior quarter. It looks backward.

When a quarterly statement illustrates *forward* as well as backward, it becomes a *lifetime statement.*

Lifetime statements can include various types of illustrations. They can often be customized to a specific plan. A lifetime statement can project an employee's ultimate account value at retirement. It might adjust this amount against an assumed inflation rate. It can even take the ultimate value and illustrate it as an income stream.

Lifetime statements can illustrate the effect that increasing deferrals can have on future account values. Various deferral and investment returns can be modeled, to help develop strategies to meet an individual's retirement "number."

Ask your plan provider about reports that can show the future benefits of employee saving today.

Number Review:

Every employee should have a number.

An employee's number is their target accumulation goal. When invested in retirement, this number should provide the inflation-adjusted income stream needed to provide that employee's lifestyle goal.

Lifetime statements are an effective way to show employees the power of saving, investing and compounding. Lifetime statements can convert a current quarterly deferral of $750 to a future retirement number of $1.65 million. When compared to $1.65 million, a small sacrifice today seems more like an opportunity than inconvenience.

PROFESSIONAL ADVISORS

Whenever possible, a company should seek the advice of qualified financial advisors for their plan. They fulfill a fiduciary need. Financial advisors can help sponsors implement their investment policy statement, and help deliver effective enrollment (sales) presentations.

Some financial advisors will meet individually with employees, to help them map out personal financial and retirement strategies. Advisors should have software that can run financial modeling. Customized financial modeling is an effective way to increase employee deferrals, and employee satisfaction in any retirement plan.

Chapter Forty-Five

_____R_____

Fiduciary Responsibilities Overview

FIDUCIARY RESPONSIBILITIES

Qualified plan fiduciaries have specific *obligations* to plan participants. They also have *liability* if those obligations are not met properly.

The Department of Labor has established strict guidelines for the behavior of qualified plan fiduciaries. These responsibilities have been put in place to protect the participants' money in retirement plans. The guidelines also protect plan fiduciaries against lawsuits, when followed properly.

If DOL guidelines are not followed correctly, fiduciaries can be held personally liable for any losses suffered by employees. So can the sponsoring company.

LOST OPPORTUNITIES

Losses are not always measured in actual dollar terms, but may be measured as *opportunity cost*. For example: A profit sharing plan that invests all of its assets in government bonds may be deemed to have violated fiduciary obligations by not investing (properly) in a balanced or diversified manner.

Note: It is possible for the fiduciaries of a plan, where participants have *never lost money,* to be considered in violation of their mandated responsibilities.

CONTROL PLAN FEES

The Department of Labor mandates that plan fiduciaries control and communicate plan fees to their employees. Why? Fees affect a plan's overall performance and success. If fees are too high, they can limit employee accumulations. If fees are too low, investment performance and/or plan services can suffer.

There are two types of fees—fees paid by the company and fees paid by employee funds. ERISA pays less attention to what an employer pays than what employees pay. The Department of Labor encourages employers to pay plan administration expenses.

Investment management fees are generally absorbed by employee funds.

Asset or annuity charges may be levied against assets, in addition to the fees for managing investments. These fees may be used to offset plan expenses. These charges must be kept "reasonable and competitive." They must also be communicated to employees.

As a fiduciary, you should analyze your plan's fees relative to the current marketplace. This can be done by allowing competitors to "bid" on your plan from time to time. If you use an advisor, make sure that this advisor is not padding fees to generate enhanced personal revenues. A fair profit is expected. Excess fees should not be tolerated.

The following links to the DOL web page reviewing plan fees:

http://www.dol.gov/ebsa/newsroom/fsparticipantfeerule.html

REASONABLE AND COMPETITIVE

Plan fiduciaries must ensure that the expenses levied against their plan's assets are *reasonable* and *competitive* within the 401(k) marketplace. If not, the employer or plan fiduciaries (or both) could be held liable for any excess.

For example: On May 18th, 2015, the U.S. Supreme Court ruled (unanimously) that the Edison International 401(k) trustees had violated their fiduciary responsibilities. The trustees had added three retail mutual funds to their plan. While doing this, the trustees failed to offer lower-priced, institutional shares of the same basic funds. The justices ruled that the Edison trustees were obligated to monitor the investments offered in their plan, and offer the lower-priced institutional shares, when available. The petitioners (plan participants) were awarded relief and damages. This ruling demonstrates the extreme importance of establishing proper fiduciary procedures. The following is a link to the ruling:

http://www.supremecourt.gov/opinions/14pdf/13-550_97be.pdf

Unlike Edison, most 401(k) plans do not have billions of dollars in plan assets. Most employers can't afford to offer low-priced institutional shares, or avoid asset charges. This is okay. But employers must still adhere to their fiduciary obligations, and establish why certain plan expense, fee and investment decisions are made.

Tibble versus Edison demonstrates that proper fiduciary conduct **must** be followed. If proper procedures are not taken, fiduciaries (and companies) can be subject to fines, including the loss of their own retirement accounts.

Fines in the past were (usually) caused by gross negligence or self-dealing. The Tibble v Edison ruling has changed that, by paving the road for litigation attorneys to attack lax fiduciaries. Be forewarned. Be diligent.

AUDIT—LIKE THE IRS

The Department of Labor can audit a retirement plan at any time. If an audit occurs, there are items that plan fiduciaries must have access to at all times. There are also items that a fiduciary must have in place at all times. Ignorance is not a defense.

DOL examiners understand that managing a 401(k) plan is complicated, and that most fiduciaries are non-professionals. However, examiners do want to see that competent experts are hired to help execute the plan and protect employee funds.

When examiners compare a plan's Form 5500, and other IRS filings, to the actual plan experience, they want to see accuracy. When they review a plan's investments, fees and education, they want to see that appropriate efforts were made to offer a competitive plan and to communicate it effectively. Neither the DOL, nor the IRS want to make regulations so onerous that employers stop offering retirement plans.

Examiners *are* concerned that fiduciaries act in the best interest of employees. If fiduciaries are acting in good faith, they are protected from fines and penalties.

It is not unusual for an auditor to suggest corrections to mistakes in a plan, without penalty. However, if fiduciaries shirk their duties, offer a poor plan, or outsource responsibilities they are required to do themselves, sparks (and fines) can fly.

Fiduciary obligations are *not* Herculean. They are stated clearly. They assure that plan participants have a plan with reasonable expenses, competitive investments and certain minimum services.

Fiduciaries must ensure that their plan remains competitive within the marketplace. They must avoid self-dealing, or un-just favoritism to a family member or an unqualified golfing buddy. Employees must have ample opportunity to learn about their plan's features, education, investments, and be made aware of all expenses.

Many administrative functions of a 401(k) can be provided by others. But there are certain responsibilities that company management cannot hand off to someone else. You must learn these responsibilities and follow them strictly. They are de-tailed in the following chapter.

INDEPENDENT FIDUCIARY RESOURCES

Managing a 401(k) plan is not easy. Companies need help to ensure a plan runs properly. You may already know competent professionals that can help you perform your fiduciary duties.

If not, independent advice can be found through the SPARK Institute.

http://www.sparkinstitute.org/contact-us.php

SPARK is a member-driven organization funded by profes-sionals in the business of 401(k) management and administra-tion.

RFP

The SPARK institute regularly creates a standardized Request For Proposal (RFP) for its members. This can be used to solicit proposals to help companies manage, change, or implement a plan. You can contact SPARK to obtain the names of members in your local area. If you schedule interviews with a number of SPARK members, or advisors who work with them, you should be able to begin the fiduciary process effectively.

FEES & EXPENSES—HOW THEY ARE PAID

Everybody that helps you must earn a profit. They should get paid, because you need their services. They earn their money in different ways.

Some providers bill direct fees to plan sponsors. These are known as *hard costs*. Hard costs are not assessed against employee investment accounts. They are paid by employers.

Other service providers get paid from assets inside a plan. These may be in the form of commissions, 12b-1 fees, asset charges or other fees passed to the consultants/advisors from investments in the plan. When expenses are paid from employee assets, they are known as *soft costs*. Plan expenses that are paid from plan assets must be disclosed to employees. They must be reasonable and competitive.

Plan and fee structures using *any* of these methods can be appropriate and competitive in the 401(k) marketplace. Soft costs should be managed in the best interest of plan participants.

Chapter Forty-Six

R

Required Fiduciary Duties

FIDUCIARY RESPONSIBILITIES UNDER ERISA

The following is a list of the basic fiduciary responsibilities that <u>all</u> fiduciaries must follow.

- Defined Contribution Plans must have a written **Statement of Investment Policy.** Think of this as a business plan for your retirement plan. The Investment Policy Statement (IPS) explains what the plan trustees and fiduciaries will do, when they will do it, and how they will do it.

- Fiduciaries must **Document** the Process of choosing **Recordkeepers & Administrators, Advisors & Investments** for the plan. This should include a *due diligence report* on each outside firm or advisor working with and for the plan.

- Accurate **Recordkeeping and Administration** must be provided for the plan.

228 — McSweeney & McGowan

- Prudent **Experts** must be engaged to help make investment decisions.

- Fiduciaries must exercise **Due Diligence** to control **Investment and Plan Expenses**.

- The plan must have a **Diversified Portfolio of Investment Choices,** determined by the **Risk/Return** objectives of the plan and its investment policy.

- The **Performance of all Money Managers must be Monitored**, and should be compared against other money managers with similar objectives and style. Investments must also be compared against the appropriate indexes.

- The important characteristics of all **Plan Investments** must be properly **Communicated** to employees. This includes **Standardized Performance** information and accurate **Fee Disclosures**.

- Assets must be held in a **Trust** (or annuity contract) that protects employee funds from outside forces.

- Trustees (and company management) must avoid **Conflicts of Interest**.

If you are involved with the management of your company's 401(k), you should understand all of the fiduciary responsibilities that are mandated by law.

Here is a link to the Department of Labor's outline of fiduciary obligations. It is followed by a link to similar information provided by the IRS.

http://www.dol.gov/ebsa/publications/fiduciaryresponsibility.html

http://www.irs.gov/Retirement-Plans/Retirement-Plan-Fiducia-ry-Responsibilities

Who Is A Fiduciary?

Over the years, the Department of Labor has issued statements regarding who might be considered a fiduciary. The DOL has cast a broad fiduciary net, which may now be interpreted to include many individuals involved with each plan. If there is any doubt, you should ask experts if you might be considered a fiduciary. Better to be safe than sorry.

Here is the fiduciary definition given by the DOL.

"Many of the actions involved in operating a plan make the person or entity performing them a fiduciary. Using discretion in administering and managing a plan or controlling the plan's assets makes that person a fiduciary to the extent of that discretion or control. Thus, fiduciary status is based on the **functions performed for the plan***, not just a person's title.*

"A plan must have at least one fiduciary (a person or entity) named in the written plan, or through a process described in the plan, as having control over the plan's operation. The named fiduciary can be identified by office or by name. For some plans, it may be an administrative committee or a company's board of directors.

"A plan's fiduciaries will ordinarily include the trustee, investment advisers, all individuals exercising discretion in the administration of the plan, all members of a plan's administrative committee (if it has such a committee), and those who select committee officials. *Attorneys, accountants, and actuaries generally are not fiduciaries when acting solely in* *their professional capacities. The key to determining whether an individual or an entity is a fiduciary is whether they are **exercising discretion or control over the plan.***"

EFFECTIVE FIDUCIARY MANAGEMENT

The Department of Labor's fiduciary publication lists a set of tips that every fiduciary should understand. The key tips are listed below, as written in the DOL document:

"Understanding fiduciary responsibilities is important for the security of a retirement plan and compliance with the law. The following tips may be a helpful starting point:

- Have you identified your plan fiduciaries, and are they clear about the extent of their fiduciary responsibilities?

- If participants make their own investment decisions, have you provided the plan and investment related information participants need to make informed decisions about the management of their individual accounts? Have you provided sufficient information for them to exercise control in making investment decisions?

- Are you aware of the schedule to deposit participants' contributions in the plan, and have you made sure it complies with the law?

- If you are hiring third-party service providers, have you looked at a number of providers, given each potential provider the same information, and considered whether the fees are reasonable for the services provided?

- Have you documented the hiring process?

- Are you prepared to monitor your plan's service providers?

- Have you identified parties in interest to the plan and taken steps to monitor transactions with them?

- Are you aware of the major exemptions under ERISA that permit transactions with parties-in-interest, especially those key for plan operations (such as hiring service providers and making plan loans to participants)?

- Have you reviewed your plan document in light of current plan operations and made necessary updates? After amending the plan, have you provided participants with an updated SPD (Summary Plan Description) or SMM (Summary of Material Modifications)?

- Do those individuals handling plan funds or other plan property have a fidelity bond?"

SECTION 404(C)

Section 404(c) took effect on January 1, 1994. These "guidelines" were intended to help plan fiduciaries reduce their liability with regard to the self-directed investments in 401(k)-type plans.

The Department of Labor final ruling on the 2007 QDIA amendment to 404(c) can be found here: https://www.dol.gov/ebsa/regs/fedreg/final/07-5147.htm

The main aspects of 404(c) regulation, and the steps you should take to ensure that your plan complies with the guidelines, are detailed in the following pages.

SUMMARY OF STEPS

Fiduciary liability for investment performance can be reduced if the following steps are taken:

- **Employee Choice**—At least three "core" investment choices must be offered.

- **Employee Direction**—Employees can direct where their individual funds are invested.

- **Employee Education**—Employees must be educated with regard to their investment choices.

- **Quarterly Changes**—Employees must be allowed to change their investments at least quarterly.

- **Employer Stock**—Detailed procedures must be followed with registration & education.

Choosing and Monitoring Investment Choices:

Section 404(c) does not relieve plan fiduciaries from the responsibilities of choosing *appropriate* investment choices for the plan, and *monitoring* these choices. The following is a good list to follow when dealing with the investments in your plan.

Default Instructions For 404(c):

- In order to qualify for Section 404(c) employees must be provided with specific investment instructions.

    o   A participant may sign a written agreement that indicates how participant funds will be invested in the absence of specific direction. The agreement should include instructions for various functions regarding investments in the plan. Such as:

❖ Mapping, Enrollment Forms, PIN # as an electronic signature that qualifies as an "in writing" requirement,

❖ Default to a Fixed Account/Money Market, Balanced Fund or Age-Based Model.

- Employees should be given a description of additional information available on request. The information that must be available to participants detailed shortly.

- Employees should receive instructions on how to obtain this material. This information should be in the Summary Plan Description.

- If there are any charges to employees for purchasing, selling and/or transferring assets, these must be disclosed.

- Employees must receive an explanation of how to give investment instructions, as well as any limits or restrictions on giving such instructions. This would include limits on how often transactions can be made, as well as extra fees or penalties involved with investment choices.

- All investment descriptions should include a general description of each investment portfolio, the risk/return characteristics of each choice, as well as information regarding the diversification of assets that comprise each portfolio. These should be included in quarterly reports.

- Employees should be informed that the plan is intended to comply with Section 404(c), and that plan fiduciaries may be relieved of liability for losses that result from a plan participants' investment choices & instructions. This declaration should be included in Summary Plan Description, Enrollment & Education Booklets, or Plan Prospectus.

Information to be Available on Request

- The value of a participant's account.

- Investment performance data with regard to all employee investment options, net of all expenses.

- A list of assets comprising the portfolio of an investment alternative. For a Fixed Account, this would include the underlying assets, as well as the current rate of return and term.

- Copies of reports, prospectuses and financial statements provided.

- A description of the annual operating expenses of each investment alternative. This includes transaction costs, management fees, administrative fees, 12b-1 and asset fees, and the amount they reduce a participant's rate of return.

ERISA Section 404(a)(1)(A) and (B)

In 2012, the Department of Labor's *Employee Benefits Security Administration* issued another final ruling regarding Fiduciary Obligations in 401(k)-type retirement plans. This ruling provided modern enhancements to Section 404(c).

Under this new rule, plan fiduciaries must act *"prudently, and solely in the interest of the plan's participants and beneficiaries."*

When a plan allows employees to make their own investment choices, they must regularly be *made aware of their own rights and responsibilities with regard to their investments.*

Plan sponsors (companies/trustees) must deliver sufficient *information for participants to make prudent decisions* regarding their personal accounts.

The plan administrator must provide this information to each participant (or beneficiary) in a specified manner.

Section 404(a)(1)(A) and (B) mandates that employees be given, or have access to certain information regarding:

- Fees & Expenses
- Investment Information
    - This information must be delivered in a format that is easy for employees to understand.
    - Employees must be able to easily compare investment options.
- Fiduciaries must use **standard methodologies** when calculating and disclosing expense and return information.
    - This information must be prepared in a manner that allows **"apples" to "apples"** comparisons when it comes to fees and performance.

The following pages provide a more detailed list of trustee obligations under Section 404(a)(1)(A) and (B).

This is edited from the following **DOL Fact Sheet.** The DOL has posted the Fact Sheet at this Web address:

http://www.dol.gov/ebsa/newsroom/fsparticipantfeerule.html

PLAN-RELATED INFORMATION (From the DOL Fact Sheet)

Certain plan-related information must be disclosed to all plan participants. This includes general information about the plan, how it works, and what it costs.

General Plan Information

- Information about the structure and mechanics of the plan must be disclosed to plan participants. This includes:

    - An explanation of how to give investment instructions under the plan,

    - A current list of the plan's investment options, and,

    - A description of any "brokerage windows," or similar arrangement, which enables the selection of investments beyond those designated by the plan.

Administrative Expenses Information

- An explanation of any fees and expenses, for general plan administrative services, that may be charged to, or deducted from, all individual accounts. Examples include fees and expenses for legal, accounting, and recordkeeping services.

Individual Expenses Information

- An explanation of fees and expenses that may be charged to, or deducted from, the individual account of a *specific participant* or beneficiary, based on the actions taken by *that* person. Examples include:

    ○ Fees and expenses for plan loans and,

    ○ Processing fees for qualified domestic relations orders.

The information in the above subcategories must be given to participants, *on or before* the date they can first direct their investments, and then again *annually* thereafter.

Statements of Actual Charges or Deductions

Participants must receive statements, at least quarterly, showing the dollar amount of the *plan-related fees and expenses* (whether "administrative" or "individual") *actually charged to, or deducted from, their individual accounts*, along with a *description of the services for which the charge or deduction was made.*

These specific disclosures may be included in quarterly benefit statements, as required under Section 105 of ERISA.

Investment-Related Information

Investment-related information must be disclosed to all plan participants. This includes:

Performance Data

- Participants must be provided specific information about historical investment performance.

- 1-, 5- and 10-year returns must be provided for investment options, such as mutual funds, that do not have fixed rates of return.

- For investment options that have a fixed or stated rate of return, the annual rate of return, and the term of the investment, must be disclosed.

Benchmark Information

- The name and returns, of an appropriate and comparative, broad-based securities *market index benchmark,* must be provided for investment options that do not have a fixed rate of return.

- The index performance information must include 1-, 5-, and 10-year periods, matching the Performance Data periods for plan investments.

- Investment options with fixed rates of return are not subject to this requirement.

Fee and Expense Information

- The total annual operating expenses (expressed both as a percentage of assets and as a dollar amount for each $1,000 invested) must be provided for investment options that do not a have a fixed rate of return.

- Any shareholder-type fees, or restrictions on the participant's ability to purchase or withdraw from the investment, must be provided for investment options that do not a have a fixed rate of return.

- Shareholder-type fees or restrictions, on the participant's ability to purchase or withdraw from the investment, must be provided for investment options that have a fixed rate of return.

Internet Website Address

- An Internet Web site, that is "sufficiently specific" to provide participants (and beneficiaries) detailed information about the plan's investment options, is considered *Investment-related information.*

Glossary

- A general glossary of terms, which is provided to assist participants and beneficiaries in understanding the plan's investment options, is considered investment-related information.

- An Internet Web site address that is sufficiently specific to provide access to such a glossary is considered investment-related information.

Comparative Format Requirement

- Investment-related information must be furnished to participants or beneficiaries on, or before, the date they can first direct their investments.

- The same information must be provided at least annually thereafter.

- The information must be furnished in a chart or similar format, designed to facilitate a comparison of each investment option available under the plan.

- A comparative chart model may be used by the plan administrator to illustrate a plan's investment option information. This must be provided in a comparative format, must be correctly completed, and must be presented as an appendix.

Miscellaneous

- The rule protects plan administrators from liability for the completeness and accuracy of information provided to participants. This is true *only* if the plan administrator "reasonably, and in good faith, relies upon information provided by a service provider."

- After a participant has invested in a particular investment option, s/he must be provided any materials the plan receives regarding voting, tender, or similar rights in the option.

- Upon request, the plan administrator must furnish prospectuses, underlying asset reports, financial reports, and statements of valuation for each plan investment option.

- The general disclosure regulation at 29 CFR § 2520.104b-1 applies to material furnished under this regulation. This includes the safe harbor for electronic disclosures at paragraph (c) of that regulation.

- This rule makes conforming changes to the disclosure requirements for plans that elect to comply with the existing ERISA section 404(c) regulations.

Chapter Forty-Seven

R
_____

Steps To Reduce Fiduciary Liability

Steps To Reduce Fiduciary Liability

Here is an easy set of steps that plan sponsors can use to reduce fiduciary liability.

Analyze Your Plan's Current Position

- Examine your plan's current investments and strategies.

- Make a detailed list of your plan's policies and procedures.

- Take a good look at your employee census data. Analyze employee participation, especially your non-highly paid employees.

- Compare your employee participation to optimal levels (>10%).

- Determine potential disbursements from the plan, especially the accounts of former employees.

Review And Formalize An Investment Policy

- Determine investment objectives and investment guidelines.
- Develop procedures for selecting money managers.
- Create securities guidelines.
- Establish procedures for monitoring investment performance.

Implement Your Investment Policy

- Ensure that your investment portfolio is well diversified.
- Analyze the performance of your plan investments against peers and appropriate benchmarks.
- Coordinate fund custody and brokerage services.
- Analyze fees and expenses at least annually.
- Fees and expenses should be reasonable, and competitive for the services received.
- Disclose all fees to employees.
- Review the plan marketplace regularly, to ensure that the plan remains competitive.
- Review and ensure that appropriate disclosures are being made to employees.
- Analyze your plan's Recordkeeping and Administration for effectiveness and accuracy.
- Periodically review participant education, and update at least annually.
- Consider Annual Lifetime Statements as an addition to normal Quarterly Statements.

Design An Optimal Portfolio

Qualified Financial Advisors should be utilized to help you choose and monitor your plan's investments. Your plan's trustees should select a diversified mix of investments that seek to maximize returns with regard to given risk tolerances.

Asset Allocation or Age-Based Models should be considered and implemented.

Monitor And Supervise

- Monthly investment reports should be prepared for plan administrators.
- Quarterly performance reports should be prepared for participants.
- Quarterly reports should compare the investment performance of funds against appropriate market indexes, their stated investment objectives, and against managers of similar style.

Danger Signs & Common Mistakes To Avoid

The following common mistakes can lead to problems with the Department of Labor:

- Having an inadequate (or missing) Investment Policy and Investment Policy Statement.
- Offering portfolios that are not diversified across the major asset classes and within specific asset classes.
- Employing investment managers who adhere to their own parameters rather than yours.
- Employing investment managers who are not subject

to proper due diligence procedures.

- Allowing employee assets to be managed by "non-experts," such as company executives who have other primary employment duties.

- Choosing investment managers based solely on performance, without regard to investment objectives, risk characteristics, and peer performance.

- Failing to use appropriate benchmarks for analysis and comparison.

- Failing to analyze total brokerage and custodial costs properly.

- Failing to disclose fees to employees.

- Setting unrealistic performance objectives.

- Measuring manager performance against inappropriate market indexes, rather than peer managers with similar management objectives.

- Not adequately addressing the complex issues involved with offering employer stock in a plan.

Chapter Forty-Eight

_____R_____

Benchmarks Of Investment Performance

INVESTMENT PERFORMANCE

As you choose investments for, and analyze investments within your retirement plan, you will need to know how well they perform. You may consider an equity mutual fund that has grown by *50%* over the past decade. This may look reasonable. But if the relevant index grew by *100%* during that same period, your fund won't be appropriate.

Fiduciaries must measure a plan's investment options against *peers*, and the appropriate *unmanaged indexes*. These indexes provide independent **benchmarks** that can be used to measure the *relative performance* of individual stocks, bonds, or managed accounts, like mutual funds.

If you watch the news, you will hear mention of the S&P 500 Index or the Dow Jones Industrial Average. These are unmanaged indexes of common stocks.

You will rarely hear reports on bond market indexes. This does not mean that they aren't important. They are. They usually don't inspire spectacular reporting. The media likes sensation. Stock market indexes can gain (or lose) two or three percent in a day. A single common stock might lose 10%. Indexes can gain or lose hundreds of points on a regular basis.

Major changes in bond prices rarely occur. When they do, such changes might be due to significant movement in the Consumer Price Index, rapid gains or losses with the U.S. or world economies (real or anticipated), or the expansion or constriction of monetary policy by the U.S. Federal Reserve, or other world banks, such as the European Central Bank.

Bond indexes move in tenths of a percent at a time. Even less. The yield on government debt might change by a few hundredths of a percent in a day. An interest rate change of one percent would send tidal waves through the economy, but small ripples in the news. Big institutions care about bond returns. The general public yawns.

There are many types of indexes (indices) available to investors and plan trustees. Indexes have been created to measure the performance of every major asset class. They have also been formed to measure various sub-groups of each major class.

Your plan's investment professionals should recommend the most appropriate indexes to measure the relative performance of investments in your plan.

As a trustee, you should see that your advisors recommend, at minimum, investments that conform to at least three core investment classes, as mandated by Section 404(C). An appropriate strategy would be to offer investments that mirror the investment classes of:

- Stocks,

- Bonds, &

- Cash.

Relevant Market Indexes

There are many indexes that measure the performance of domestic stocks. Some of the major indexes are explained below:

U.S. STOCKS

Large Cap:

Large cap stocks have the largest market capitalization of US equities. The indexes that measure the performance of large companies vary in structure. The companies included in these indexes tend to have market capitalization of at least $3.5 billion.

- The Dow Jones Industrial Average Index represents 30 large US industrial companies (Such as Apple, 3M, IBM, Microsoft & Wall Mart), which are chosen to represent a cross-section of American business.

- The Dow Jones Wilshire Large-Cap Index represents the "large-cap" portion of the Dow Jones Wilshire 5000 Index. This index contains the 750 largest public companies, as measured by total market capitalization.

- The S&P 500 Index represents the 500 largest publicly traded companies.

Mid-Cap:

As a general rule, mid-cap stocks have market capitalizations more than $1 billion and less than $5 billion.

- The Dow Jones Wilshire Mid-Cap Index is a subset of the The Dow Jones Wilshire 5000 Index. It consists of the US companies that are ranked 501-1,000, as measured by total market capitalization. The higher ranked companies might still be considered large-cap, while those close to a rank of 1,000 might be considered small cap companies.

- The S&P 400 Mid-Cap Index includes stocks with market capitalizations from (approximately) $750 million to about $3.5 billion.

Small Cap:

Most small-cap stocks have market capitalizations under $1 billion.

- The performance of small-cap domestic stocks is measured by the Dow Jones Wilshire US Small-Cap Index. This is comprised of stocks ranked 751-2,500 in the Wilshire Index.
- The S&P Small-Cap 600 Index measures a somewhat similar mix of small-cap stocks.
- The Russell 2000 Index measures the performance of small-cap stocks. It represents the bottom 2,000 stocks of the Russell 3000 Index.

International Stocks

The primary International Stock indexes are measured by Morgan Stanley, a large institutional Broker/Dealer firm. They are as follows:

- The MSCI EAFE Index (Europe, Asia, & Far East)
- The MSCI World

NASDAQ

The NASDAQ Index represents companies traded on the electronic NASDAQ system. These stocks often represent high tech companies. The NASDAQ Index is often used to measure the broad performance of technology companies.

Bonds

The performance of bonds is measured in a number of ways. Remember: The primary goals of bond investors are safety of principal, current income, and some potential for gain.

The major bond indexes focus around the following major index classes: Global bonds, US bonds, Government bonds, Emerging Market bonds, High-Yield bonds & Asset-Backed securities.

Within a retirement plan, bonds tend to be from two primary asset classes — government & corporate bonds. High-yield, asset-backed and international bonds may also be part of an expanded mix.

The most widely used indexes are Barclays and Lipper. You may encounter them in your research:

- The Barclays Capital Aggregate Bond Index measures a very broad mix of bonds. These bonds consist primarily of widely-traded treasury securities, government agency bonds, corporate bonds and asset-backed securities. This index is often used to measure the general performance of investment-grade bonds.
  - Barclays also has indexes that measure the performance of long-term, mid-term and short term bonds.
- Lipper (a division of Thompson Reuters) has various indexes that measure bonds by asset class, credit quality and duration.

$&C

Chapter Forty-Nine

_____R_____

Investment Policy Statement

INVESTMENT POLICY STATEMENT

An Investment Policy Statement is the business plan for the investments in your retirement plan.

While companies should hire outside professionals to help choose and monitor their plan's investments, fiduciaries must still *manage the managers*.

The following is a sample Investment Policy Statement (IPS). If possible, you should work with your plan's investment consultants and plan administrators to develop your own IPS. It should be appropriately tailored to your plan and your provider.

ABC Company, Inc. 401(k) Plan

Date

Investment Policy Statement

Plan Name: ABC Company, Inc. 401(k) Plan
ABC Company, Inc.: ABC Company, Inc.
Tax I.D. Number: 02-0000000
Type of Plan: Profit Sharing and 401(k) Plan
Date of IPS: Date

This Investment Policy Statement (**IPS**) is intended for use in connection with the ABC Company, Inc.'s Retirement Plan. ABC has engaged The Best Mutual Funds (**The Best**) to provide investment services to ABC. ABC and The Best have entered into an Investment Services Agreement. This agreement outlines the services to be provided by The Best, and ABC, in connection with ABC Company, Inc.'s tax qualified employee retirement plan (**Plan**).

This IPS shall remain in place until terminated or amended by the Plan.

The Plan trustees have appointed John Smith & Jane Doe as brokers of record/investment advisers to assist with the effective implementation of the Plan.

Purpose of the Investment Policy Statement

The purpose of this IPS is to:

- Set forth ABC Company, Inc.'s and/or the Plan Trustees' objectives for structuring a retirement savings program suitable to the long-term needs and risk tolerances of Plan participants;

- Define the roles and expectations of Plan fiduciaries;

- Define the roles and expectations of all other parties responsible for the Plan's investments;

- Formulate policies for selecting appropriate investments to be offered to Plan participants and beneficiaries covered by the Plan;

- Establish prudent procedures for monitoring and evaluating the performance of investments within the Plan;

- Establish prudent procedures for monitoring, evaluating and communicating all fees within the Plan;

- Implement and maintain an investment selection process that is integrated with the services that Plan participants receive through The Best;

- Establish procedures for educating employees about the plan features, as well as the investment options in the plan;

- Determine procedures to monitor the accounting for all investment, recordkeeping and administrative expenses associated with the Plan.

Purpose of Plan

ABC Company, Inc.'s 401(k) plan was established on January 1, xxxx to provide a retirement savings program for the employees of ABC Company, Inc. The Plan is maintained exclusively to benefit Plan participants. The Plan is intended to operate in accordance with all applicable state and federal laws and regulations.

COMPLIANCE WITH ERISA SECTION 404(c) and SECTION 404(A) (1) (A) and (B)

The Plan is intended to comply with ERISA Section 404(C) and Section 404(a) (1) (A) and (B) (and any other corresponding regulations issued by the Department of Labor), which provide a plan sponsor and other plan fiduciaries with relief from liability for the investment decisions made by participants.

The goal of the Plan is to provide a framework for ABC Company, Inc.'s employees to establish a savings and investment program for their retirement. While Plan participants are ultimately responsible for their own investment decisions, ABC Company, Inc. in conjunction with The Best and the Plan's designated investment representatives, will provide a range of investment options reasonably intended to permit Plan participants the opportunity to:

- Develop their own portfolio strategies.
- Invest in accordance with their own,
  - Retirement goals,
  - Risk tolerances, and
  - Saving and investment time horizons.

Plan Objectives

ABC Company, Inc. and the Plan Trustees, with recommendations from Smith, Doe and The Best, will select and monitor the investment options in accordance with the following objectives:

- Promote and optimize retirement wealth accumulation by Plan participants;
- Provide Plan participants with a diversified range of asset classes and investment options intended to help them meet their investment objectives;
- Establish the criteria for selecting investment options;
- Establish procedures to monitor the performance of investment options;
- Establish procedures to monitor investment costs to ensure that the Plan's investment costs remain competitive;

- Establish procedures to terminate and replace investment options and/or service providers that do not meet the Plan's established objectives.

Selection of Investment Classes

Various investment classes and asset-allocated models will be selected to provide opportunities for risk/return and diversification alternatives. The investments chosen for the Plan should reasonably accommodate the anticipated investment requirements and preferences of Plan participants.

It is ABC Company, Inc.'s intent to use the investment selection system as set forth below to aid in selecting investment options for Plan participants.

Investment funds may be selected to fill three or more of the following categories, depending upon the Plan's objectives. During the selection process, the history, performance, style and fees of each investment fund will be reviewed.

Equity Funds

Large Cap Funds – Value, Blend, Growth

Mid Cap Funds – Value, Blend, Growth

Small Cap Funds – Value, Blend, Growth

International and Global Equity Funds – Value, Blend, Growth

Aged-based Models

Asset Allocation Models

- Aggressive Growth
- Moderate Growth
- Conservative Growth
- Capital Preservation

Fixed Income Funds

High Quality Short Term, Intermediate Term, and Long-Term Government Bond Funds

Medium Quality Short Term, Intermediate Term, and Long-Term Government Bond and General Bond Funds

Asset-Backed Bond Funds

High Yield Bond Funds

Money Market Fund/Stable Value Funds

Investment Selection System

The Plan will select investment options from The Best's program menu. The Plan trustees will consider the following criteria in selecting particular investment options for the program. They shall apply only at the time of selection of the investment fund, unless otherwise specified below. The criteria do not apply to the selection of Index Funds.

Each investment option should meet each of the following criteria:

INVESTMENT MANAGER

- It may be an Investment Management Company that is registered under the Investment Company Act of 1940.
- It may be a Registered Investment Adviser registered under the Investment Adviser Act of 1940.
- It may be an insurance company.
- It may be a bank.

DUE DILIGENCE

- The investment issuer must be in good standing with industry, federal and state regulators.

- The investment issuer must satisfy the Investment Committee's Due Diligence, and must provide detailed additional information regarding the following:

  o A history of the firm;

  o The management of the firm;

  o The firm's financial status;

  o The firm's management style, philosophy and approaches to investment selection;

  o The firm's primary and local servicing locations;

  o All relevant fee schedules and information.

Preliminary Review

Fund History

Each Large Cap domestic investment fund is required to have a minimum of five years of investment history.

Small Cap and Mid Cap Domestic Equity Investment Funds and Foreign Equity Investment Funds are required to have at least three years of operating history.

The Plan recognizes that some "retirement shares," "asset allocation models," or "aged-based models" might be a special class of shares designed for retirement plans. These funds may have operating histories that may not meet the criteria for traditional, retail funds.

Retirement shares or models may be utilized if such funds can meet the Plan's investment criteria by demonstrating qualifying performance by the underlying managers, funds, indexes, or management teams. The Plan may consider alternative historical time frames for other classes of shares for the same fund, provided that the fund is substantially similar except for the share type classification.

Relative Performance

Each Large Cap domestic investment fund is expected to have performed in or near the top half of its investment category on either a three or five-year basis. The Plan expects each fund to maintain at least a neutral Morningstar Rating™ for either a three or five year basis. The Plan may elect to utilize other fund evaluation companies, such as Lipper. The Lipper Rating should be at least three stars for a three, five or ten-year time frame.

Small Cap and Mid Cap domestic equity investment funds and Foreign equity investment funds are expected to have at least a three or five-year rank near or above the top half of their category, and maintain at least a neutral Morningstar Rating™. The Plan may elect to utilize other fund evaluation companies, such as Lipper. The Lipper Rating should be at least three stars for a three, five, or ten-year time frame.

It is understood that there may be times when particular funds underperform their peers on a three or five year basis. If this event occurs, such fund will be placed on a "watch" list. The Plan Trustees will discuss this investment choice with The Plan's outside investment experts. If there is no reasonable explanation for the fund's underperformance, such fund shall be replaced by a fund that meets The Plan's requirements. If the fund's *long-term performance* (10-year) is still above average,

The Plan Trustees are authorized to keep the fund in the program, provided there is a reasonable expectation that the fund will return to its traditional, relative performance levels.

Manager Tenure

Each investment fund must have had the same portfolio manager, or a member of the same management team, in place for at least the previous three years. If neither is present, the performance of the manager (or team) may be analyzed for prior performance with other fund(s). New managers with no prior track record will not be acceptable.

Due to the reduced history requirement for Small Cap and Mid Cap Domestic equity funds and Foreign equity investment funds, prior portfolio manager tenure is reduced to a minimum of two years for this category.

Exceptions to this rule are allowed on a case-by-case basis, but it is required that the majority of The Plan's investment choices will adhere to these criteria.

Incidents that may cause such exceptions may include:

- An existing management team, or manager, that meets The Plan's expectations, takes over the management of a fund.
- If experienced manager(s) are starting a new fund, utilizing their prior track record will be allowed by the Plan.

Minimum Assets

Large cap investment funds are expected to have a minimum of two hundred million dollars in assets under management. Small cap and mid cap domestic and foreign equity investment funds, are expected to have minimum assets of one hundred million dollars.

Expenses

Each of the Plan's investment funds are expected to have over-all expense ratios that are no more than 25% above the average expense ratio for the respective investment fund category. The average total Plan investment expense shall be no more than 20% above the average expense ratios for similar funds in re-tirement plans of similar size.

The Plan is allowed to incur asset charges or fees, in addition to fund expenses, provided they are reasonable and in line with other 401(k) plans with similar characteristics.

All fund expenses must be disclosed to each participant in the Plan.

Adherence to Style

All funds shall be monitored to ensure that they are managed according to the fund's stated style objectives. Funds that de-viate from their stated style shall be placed on "watch," and shall be replaced for that category if the fund does not return to its stated style objective within one calendar year.

Final Review

The Plan's trustees shall meet with The Plan's investment ex-perts at least annually to review The Plan's investment offer-ings. Attention will be given to such items as an investment's Sharpe ratio, style consistency, standard deviation, alpha, beta and percentage of calendar years above median performance. The Plan trustees will replace funds that consistently fail to meet the expectations in this IPS.

The performance of models shall be analyzed based upon their relative percentage of underlying assets. Models shall also be analyzed relative to other models with similar objectives.

Monitoring of Investment Options

The Plan's investment funds will be monitored, as reasonably necessary, to permit the Investment Committee to evaluate any material changes to an investment fund's operation or performance. All investment funds, with the exception of Index Funds, are expected to maintain the minimum criteria established in the selection process, subject to the following exceptions:

Relative Performance

Once selected, each large cap fund is expected to maintain a minimum of average performance in its investment category on a three-year or five year basis. The Plan expects each fund to maintain at least a neutral Morningstar Rating™ for either a three or five year basis. With Lipper, this is a rating of 3. The fund is also expected to perform in the top 50% of funds, within its investment category, for three out of the past five years, or six out of the last ten years.

Small cap funds, mid cap funds, and foreign equity investment funds are not required to have a five year record. They are expected to maintain at least a neutral Morningstar Rating™ for either a three or five year basis. With Lipper, this is a rating of 3.

Models shall be analyzed for effectiveness based upon their underlying assets, not their stated objectives. For example: If a model is composed of 30% large-cap stocks, 10% mid-cap stocks, and 60% corporate bonds, the model performance shall be compared (as is reasonably possible) to a hypothetical fund comprised of a similar percentage of asset class indexes.

Performance is expected to be in, or above, the third quintile over the most recent three or five-year time frame. Alternatively, such models may be analyzed against other models with similar objectives and asset class distribution. Models are expected to be at or above average for either a three, five, or ten-year time frame. They are expected to maintain at least a neutral rating with Morningstar, or a rating of 3 stars with Lipper.

Manager Tenure

When an investment fund manager leaves a fund, the new manager shall be researched. The manager's previous track record will be evaluated. The mere fact that a manager disassociates from an investment fund will not require that such investment fund be eliminated from the Plan's funds, particularly where the fund has a team of managers. Any replacement manager(s) shall be evaluated upon prior performance, as defined earlier in this IPS. Such manager(s) must meet the Plan's minimum performance criteria regarding prior performance.

Fund Analysis and Removal

ABC Company, Inc., will work with Smith and Doe to analyze materials from The Best, Morningstar, Lipper, or similar rating services to analyze each mutual fund company. A review of each investment offering shall be conducted at least annually. The monitoring process will be facilitated by services provided by The Best, Morningstar, Lipper, or a similar rating service, and Smith and Doe.

The Plan trustees may recommend removal of investment funds that underperform, change investment objectives, experience management and organizational changes, or present other questions or concerns.

The Best may remove funds from its offering menu. The Best may also place certain investment funds on a "watch list" for future monitoring until a definitive determination can be made by ABC Company, Inc. 401(k) Plan trustees and/or The Best with respect to such investment funds.

Default Fund Options

Retirement plan fiduciaries must designate an investment option to be used as a default fund for plan participants who do not make a specific investment election upon enrolling in the plan.

The Investment Committee will establish a default investment option. The Committee shall follow ERISA Section 404(c), the prudent investor rule, and the final QDIA guidelines published by the Department of Labor to determine this default investment option.

The default option shall be a "balanced fund" or an appropriate age-based model for each plan participant.

A balanced fund should be composed of an approximate allocation of sixty percent stocks and forty percent bonds and cash. This is determined to be a prudent selection for a default fund investment. The equity portion of the default fund may be representative of the broad equity markets. It may also consist primarily of large-cap U.S. equities, provided this still represents a mix of asset classes. The bond portion shall attempt to approximate the performance of the broad fixed income markets, such as those measured by the Barclays Capital Aggregate Bond Index. It may also be a broad blend of U.S. government and/or U.S. corporate bonds.

If aged-based models are utilized by the plan, a model based upon each participant's current age, shall considered an appropriate default investment choice.

PLAN DOCUMENT

This IPS is intended to coordinate with the Plan Document. Any recognized conflicts shall be analyzed, and corrected wherever possible.

Investment or ABC Company, Inc. Committee Members:

Name	Date
Name	Date
Name	Date
Name	Date
Name	Date

$&C

Chapter Fifty

R

Book Summary

Employers can utilize many different types of retirement plans, in various combinations. The appropriate mix for a company will be determined by its particular needs.

This book gives employers an overview of the uses and benefits of each major retirement plan option, and how it might be used.

Don't be afraid to ask your plan consultants to extend themselves for your benefit. There are often better ways to accomplish your objectives.

If you are an executive in charge of your company's retirement plan(s), think about how you can take the information here and put it to good use. Seek better solutions. They are usually available.

TARGETED BENEFITS

If you wish to implement plans that favor ownership or company management, you have different strategies at your disposal. You can implement plans that are "qualified" for preferential tax treatment, or plans that are "non-qualified."

Because of their tax and asset-protection benefits, qualified plans will often be your first choice.

Non-qualified benefits, such as deferred compensation and split dollar life insurance, can be used to supplement qualified plans. Selective benefits are especially useful for attracting and retaining key executives.

PLANS FOR ALL

Qualified plans must be offered to all eligible employees. Some treat employees the same. Others treat employees the "same," but with subtleties that allow for the skewing of company contributions toward senior management and/or ownership.

401(K)

The most popular qualified retirement benefit is a 401(k). 401(k)s are popular with employees because:

- They are an easy way to save.

- They allow employees to plan for retirement in a tax-favored manner.

- Employees control their own investment accounts.

- Employees may benefit from matching contributions.

Employers like 401(k) plans because:

- They are cost-effective.

- They help attract and retain quality employees.

- Employee wealth accumulation creates greater productivity.

- 401(k)s help maintain higher job satisfaction.

In today's business marketplace, no company should be without a 401(k).

401(k)s must be implemented for all eligible employees. They may or may not include a matching contribution.

UNUSUAL APPROACH

This book has approached 401(k) design and implementation in an important, but non-traditional manner.

Human emotions, instincts, and our internal nature are powerful forces that compel behavior.

Emotions drive us toward positive outcomes. They can drive us to negative outcomes, and sabotage our ability to plan for a secure retirement.

This book shows you how to design a 401(k) that accommodates natural behavior. It explains methods that can turn human nature into your employees' best ally, not their worst financial adversary. This results in greater plan participation and better investment results.

Making 401(k) enhancements will help more employees achieve their optimum outcome—true financial independence at retirement.

You may need a few small tweaks to your planning. You may need a complete overhaul of your plan's design and information architecture to achieve success.

Finally, this book shows you how to protect your company, and its plan fiduciaries, against regulatory punishment and employee lawsuits.

You know the facts. Now, set your goals and take the steps to achieve them.

As you review your 401(k) architecture, keep these ideas in mind.

- Employees need your help.

- Simply offering a 401(k) plan is not enough.

EDUCATION IS CRITICAL

Proper 401(k) education is crucial. Without the right education, your employees will never reach their full financial potential. Every education program should help employees:

1. Understand the importance of saving today.

2. Determine how much they must save to achieve their financial goals.

3. Become compelled to take action. Saving and investing more will reduce stress, not cause it.

4. Choose an investment strategy that meets their financial and emotional needs.

5. Remain invested through the inevitable market downturns.

6. Adapt as they age.

7. Keep faith as the social and financial world evolves rapidly.

Good luck as you continue the challenges of employee retirement. It isn't easy. But it is very worthwhile. Hopefully, this book will help.

BOOK
INDEX

www.ingramcontent.com/pod-product-compliance
Lightning Source LLC
Chambersburg PA
CBHW070736270326
41927CB00010B/2018